JEREMIAH 29:11
THE PLANS I   HAVE FOR YOU, WOMAN:
WALK IN VICTORY!

Written by: Dr. Brandi DeShawn Brown

Edited by: Courtney Berry
Iron *PROOF* Editing Firm

I0158624

Dr. Brandi DeShawn Brown

2016 ISBN 978-0-9896965-0-0 Jeremiah 29:11 The Plans I Have For You Woman: Walk In Victory!

Jeremiah 29:11 Ministries/School Street Counseling and Consulting Services Rockford, Illinois 61101

Book Cover Illustration by Kenneth Crawford of KDawg Production

Contents

Dedication

To my children Carandus Junior, Jamaia, and Imani. I love you all.

To:My mother, Penny Ann (John) Devereueawax,
     Father, George B. Bacon II
     Grandparents, Jim and Novella Johnson
     Uncle Harold (Katy) Johnson, Author of, *Revelation of God*
     Aunt Ann Cox for love and the foundation to seek the Lord.

To all my brothers and sisters, nieces and nephews. I love you all.
Believe in Jeremiah 29:11 because God has Plans for You!!!

My children's Godparents and families
     Leonard and Dennia James, Diona (Rob), Monica (Mark),
     Jocelyn, Michael, Darious, and Darnell

     Benny Sr. and Linda Crawford, Benny Crawford Jr., Promise,
     LaToya, and Kenny Crawford

     Minister Dorthory Wright

To my family matriarchs: Ethel Johnson, Moma Della, and Rev.
     Mattie Harris, and Vera Bacon for setting the Jeremiah 29:11
     foundation in our families and communties.

To the late, Rev. Dr. Floyd Prude for always "picking me up!"
     To Mrs. Regina Prude, whose smile is from the Lord.

Thank you. Without your support and patience to achieve this dream.

Special dedication to Sister Rosie Blake, God has plans for you!

Acknowledgements

I would like to thank and acknowledge my writing editor, Courtney Berry. Thank you so much for sharing your writing and editing gifts in this project. You are such a blessing. Blessings to you.

My spiritual mentor and cousin, Charlyne Blatcher Martin, for working closely as a consultant for writing these books.I looked forward to each meeting with you.

Rev. Chester and Mrs. Doris Baker, Antar Baker, Baker family for spiritual and educational consulting during this writing journey.

My sister Domonique S. Devereueawax for early editing.

My Pastor, Charlene Bulls-Mills and Allen Chapel A.M.E. Church Rockford, Illinois.

Jonathan Devereueawax, Jocelyn James, Nicole Reed, and Amari Spates for being an answered prayer!

Without your help and prayers this book process and completion. Thank you for your patience and guidance throughout this project.

Love, BB

Foreword I

Dr. Brandi Brown asked that I consult with her about a series of books that she had in progress. From the first time we met, I noticed her total commitment to doing God's Work as she had been directed. Dr. Brown was on a divine mission honed by experiences that may have stopped someone who was not listening for God's Answers to her questions. Her determination to do this work resonated with my belief that God chooses who He wants to do a particular task. Dr. Brown was chosen to write *The Plans I Have For You, Woman: Walk in Victory.* She said, "Yes."

The purpose of the book is to speaks to women discovering and doing what God planned for us all along; Jeremiah 29:11 - "For I know the plans I have for you declares the Lord, plans to prosper you and not to harm you, plans to give you hope and a future."

Dr. Brown's walk through Jeremiah 29:11 gives you a guided step-by-step tour of how to discover the path to fulfill your destiny as a God-guided woman in every aspect of your life. It doesn't stop with the discovery. This book takes you by the hand and gives you the tools to reach higher than you may have dared to dream. It shows you how to use the tools in an easy to understand manner. With a desire to become the woman that God created, your Bible, and this book, your journey can become more than a dream. *The Plans I Have For You, Woman* will lift your level of realization as to how important you are to God, yourself, your family, and all who come into your path. You will discover and rejoice in what it means to be "chosen" and to become "victorious!"

Charlyne Blatcher Martin, M.A.
Consultant and Television Talk Show Host of
'Something to Talk About'

Foreword II

I had the privilege of helping to edit and read *The Plans I Have For You, Woman: Walk in Victory* as Dr. Brown was preparing it to be published. This book captures the true essence of the personal struggles and crossroads of women young and old. It allows you to find your story and identify with the ageless stories of women in the Bible that God uses to show his everlasting love and eternal promise of hope, help, and hand of favor. The wisdom, insight, and inspiration gives one the hope to believe God has a purpose and assignment for life if you walk it out and work it out. Then, for sure, you will walk in victory!

Penny Devereueawax

Introduction

The purposes of this book

My prayer is that this book brings you the light and hope needed to prosper in the plans God has for you. God designed you with a purpose to succeed in every situation when you stay connected according to Jeremiah 29:11. You have what it takes to grow spiritually in situations by understanding your promise.

First, let's take a look at the prophet Jeremiah. Jeremiah spoke God's messages to the generations of Israel to spiritually prepare them to uproot move from their homeland Jerusalem to Babylon. This move required the children of Israel to transition by taking their spirituality, traditions and customs, people, leaders and Levites, and personal belongings to live as residents in a different culture. This new culture was Babylon—a land where people lived without Godly principles and worshiped false gods. It was important for the Israelites to keep their faith in their God while living in and among the people of Babylon.

Secondly, God gave Jeremiah instructions for these generations to follow while living as captives in Babylon. The major instructions in Jeremiah's message were 1) turn to God 2) fear the Lord and 3) live out Godly principles. It's important to understand that God is fair and just in the plans and purposes of your life to reach your next level. The Nation of Israel, which exited Egypt, disobeyed God and was not allowed to enter into the Promised Land. The enemy does not want you to discover Jeremiah 29:11 plans and purpose. The plan of the enemy is to keep you distracted from discovering God's plan for you. The children of the first generation entered the Promised Land when their grandparents and parents died. Moses was the leader of this first generation that exited Egypt and wandered for forty years in the wilderness. His responsibility was to lead this generation into the Promise Land; however, he lost the privilege to enter and lead the next generations into their new land. His responsibility became building the Ark of Covenant and delegating authority to teach and train the generations how to live in the plans God had for His people.

Thereafter, the generations continued to multiply and grow even though some turned to worship idles and intermarried with other clans. As a result, the Nation of Israel lived in and out of captivity under the suppression of stronger countries. God continued to raise up individual prophets, leaders, and followers to carry out His plans for the next generations. Jeremiah was a prophet in a time when the tribes became scattered and the people depended on the king.

The goal of this book is to help you prepare and transition yourself and the people in your household, family, and community for their assigned Jeremiah 29:11 plans and purposes. Hope and Faith are key principles for walking in your Jeremiah 29:11 identity. Let me encourage you to have hope in your situation and not to fear your enemy because you have a promise. Pray and trust God right now where you are because you have a purpose and promise! While in exile, Jeremiah delivered many messages to the elders, priest, prophets, and all the people about God's promise, protection, and plan

One of the letters to these people read:

The Lord Almighty, the God of Israel, sends this message to all the captives he has exiled to Babylon from Jerusalem: (5) Build homes, and plan to stay. Plant gardens, and eat the food you produce. (6) Marry, and have children. Then find spouses for them, and have many grandchildren. Multiply! Do not dwindle away! (7) And work for the peace and prosperity of Babylon. Pray to the Lord for that city where you are held captive for if Babylon has peace, so will you." (8) The Lord Almighty, the God of Israel, says, "Do not let the prophets and mediums who are there in Babylon trick you. Do not listen to their dreams (9) because they prophesy lies in my name. I have not seen them," says the Lord. (10) The truth is that you will be in Babylon for seventy years. But then I will come and do for you all the good things I have promised, and I will bring you home again.

(11) For I know the plans I have for you," says the Lord. "They are plans for good and not for disaster, to give you a future and a hope. (12) In those days when you pray, I will listen. (13) If you look for me in earnest, you will find me when you seek me. (14) I will be found by you," says the Lord. "I will gather you out of the nations where I sent you and bring you home again to your own land."

Another purpose of this book is to share with you Jeremiah's message that God has plans for you to have hope in your right now situations and future--especially in obstacles. The children of Israel faced obstacles as they transitioned from Jerusalem to Babylon. God's promises and hope for you are to have peace in your situations and move forward in your plans. While in Babylon, the people of God were protected and prosperous. After seventy years, the people and their children's generation left Babylon and returned back to their inherited land. They returned back with their belongings and built their homes. The generations who returned home became witnesses to God's plans and promise to return. I believe these people remained hopeful for God's plans to multiply, have hope, and prosper in the will of God. Today, women need to know their inherited Jeremiah 29:11 plans to prosper, wait, and harvest in their spiritual life.

God's Plan for Women: PROSPER

Prosperity is in your future. Woman of God, understand that you are designed to give birth, create, and produce life in your Jeremiah 29:11 assignment. As women, we have to continually pray and plant the Word of God into our household, spouse, children, and field placements. Throughout this book, you will read about women who prospered in the Lord by increasing their faith. Walking by faith (II Corinthians 5:7) is a continual theme throughout this book. Therefore, it is hoped that you will build your hope on things eternal and remember that you were made in the image of God. Knowing this makes you an overcomer as you face obstacles. Let me encourage you to be like the farmer and plant your seed (new information) in good ground and wait for your harvest to grow. You have to learn how to be a planter. This means that you have to spiritually grow and mature in the Lord while you walk on your Jeremiah 29:11 path.

God's Plan for Women: PLANT

God's plan for women is to plant their seed into good ground. A farmer is an overseer of the crops growing on the land. The farmer's duty is to be responsible for the seed's growth in good ground. Farmers have a responsibility to learn about the seasons, ground, weather temperature, and the seed to plant. The seed is God's message; however, the Devil wants to steal it and prevent it from producing fruit. God wants you to cling to His message and steady produce a huge harvest (Luke 8:5-15). It is important that you evaluate your environment and people you keep as your company this season.

You were designed with the Jeremiah 29:11 seed which is God's message and purpose for your life. It is time for you to hear the message because the Devil wants to come and steal it away and prevent you from believing and being saved. You need to be like a young plant and hear the message with joy so your roots will go very deep in the Word. You will need deep roots in the Word to be able to stand the obstacles that will arise to shake up your faith. The plans God has for you are to stand in good ground and hear and accept the message so you can mature into your Jeremiah 29:11 assignment. God wants you to produce good and honest hearts and to embrace His message. God made you to cling to Him and steadily produce a huge harvest.

The Jeremiah 29:11 plans God has for you were made and spoke out into existence from the womb of God. This means there is a Jeremiah 29:11 seed planted in you. There is a command from the mouth of God—a word, a prophecy spoken over your life to prosper in God's will. You must get connected to this seed in you. Let me encourage you to be like the farmer that sought the Lord's wisdom and plant the seeds of faith to discover the treasures in your Jeremiah 29:11 identities while in prayer. Remember to remain in the vineyard's court and connected to the vine! Everything you need: your miracle, joy, peace, understanding, wisdom, love, happiness, and healing is in the Lord's vineyard's court.

God's Plan for Women: WAIT

Learn to listen and wait as you seek to understand the secrets of the seeds. While you wait, you need to pray, fast, believe, and have great faith. It's going to rain, but God has you covered. Begin to thank God in your secret place of praying for your children and the Kingdom treasures He has given you. Go into your secret place in prayer while you wait. This secret place is discovered in Psalm 91:1.

Psalm 91:1 Those who live in the shelter of the Most High will find rest in the shadow of the Almighty.

While you continue to wait, you need to sow and grow into your harvest. Your harvest is the fruit of the Spirit that you produce through a relationship with Jesus. You can pray, study, and surround yourselves with wise people this season as you discover your Jeremiah 29:11 identities.

God's Plan for Women: REAP a HARVEST

Be willing to listen to wisdom so you will grow spiritually and mature in the Lord. As you mature, you should surround yourselves with wise people and become confident in the plans God has for you. Your job is to identify and learn your assignments and seasons and evaluate people. Thank Him for spring buds, sprouts, and new growth in your field. Begin to plow weeds and allow God to remove the figs out of your field. You do not want to be like the fig tree that withered up.

Matthew 21: (18) In the morning, as Jesus was returning to Jerusalem, he was hungry, (19) and he noticed a fig tree beside the road. He went over to see if there were any figs on it, but there were only leaves. The he said to it, "May you never bear fruit again!" And immediately the fig tree withered up. (20) The disciples were amazed when they saw this and asked, "How did the fig tree withered up. (21) Then Jesus told them, "I assure you, you can do things like this and much more. You can even say to this mountain, "May God lift you up and throw you into the sea, and it will happen. (22) If you believe, you will receive whatever you ask for in prayer."

Believe and conceive that God has plans for you. My sisters, please pray with expectations. Be a producer of the fruits of the Spirit by staying connected to Jesus, the True Vine. You are responsible for your gifts and talents when you discover your Jeremiah 29:11 identity. Therefore, it is important that you examine the people your crowds, environments, and thoughts this season.

Still Point and Still Point Moments and Still Point Reflections

The following is a preface for this book and a guide for Still Point Moments and Reflections. The Word of God tells us to be silent and be still. Let me empower you with two Still Moment scriptures:

1. *Be silent, and know that I am God! I will be honored by every nation. I will be honored throughout the world (Psalm 46:10).*

2. *He that is unjust, let him be unjust still: and he which is filthy, let him be filthy still: and he that is righteous still: and he that is holy, let him be holy still (Revelation 22:11).*

In the plans God has for you, God wants you to be still. As you read, you will come across **Still Point Scriptures (SPS), Moments (MT), and Reflections (RF)** to have devotion. Each chapter will open with SPS and prayer to begin your chapter reflection. This reflection means to ponder, meditate, give back, or show an image. As you reflect in your SPS be sure to mediate on the scriptures and God's purpose and plan. Devotion is the noun form of devote which means to consecrate, dedicate, or to give up something. Devotion can also mean to attach to a cause or person, to consecrate, dedicate, or to give up something. God wants us to devote our time, that He has blessed us with, back to Him. Devotion is your one-on-one time with God. Devote time to be silent and still to hear the plans for you. Fellowship with God requires a focus on discovering your purpose. Are you ready to follow God? There are many followers of Jesus in this book who devoted their means and time to live according to the Word. As you read SPSs, MTs, and RFs, you, too, will devote moments to reflect and have devotions on your Jeremiah 29:11 plans.

The end of each chapter will include **Still Point Reflections (SPR).** Reflections here mean deep thought or an indirect approach. The SPR is your moment to have devotion, deep thought, and an indirect approach to stay on the path God has prepared for you. Still point scriptures, moments, and reflections are designed for you to examine your situation and give it to Jesus. Let's examine this scripture from *Mark 4:38:-41:*

(35) As evening came, Jesus said to his disciples, "Let's cross to the other side of the lake." (36) He was already in the boat, so they started out, leaving the crowds behind (although other boats followed). (37) But soon a fierce storm arose. High waves began to break into the boat until it was nearly full of water.

(38) Jesus was sleeping at the back of the boat with his head on a cushion. Frantically they woke him up, shouting. "Teacher, don't you even care that we are going to drown?" (39) When he woke up, he rebuked the wind and said to the water, "Quiet down!" Suddenly the wind stopped, and there was a great calm. (40) And he asked them, "Why are you so afraid? Do you still not have faith in me?" (41) And they were filled with awe and said among themselves, "Who is this man, that even the wind and waves obey him?"

God is the Father of time and our seasons and He knows what you are going through physically, emotionally, and spiritually. God wants you to have faith in Him no matter what the situation looks like. Beloved, please understand that you are a witness for the goodness and mercy of God. This means that you are God's vessel to be used on Earth for the Kingdom. Your life has been preordained for you to experience victory after victory and glory to glory. Indeed, you are a witness for God's glory in your life just as the followers of Christ in scriptures. More specifically, you are a witness how God intervened supernaturally and changed *your* life.

The disciples witnessed firsthand the miracles Jesus performed. They witnessed Jesus *"heal a man with a deformed hand (Mark 3:1). Also, Jesus and his disciples went out to the lake, followed by a huge crowd from all over Galilee, Judea (Mark 3:7), (8) Jerusalem, Idumea, from east of the Jordan River, and even from as far away as Tyre and Sidon."* They were witnesses to Jesus' miracles and teachings just as you. You are the seed that God is watching over (Jeremiah 1:12). Faith in God is the key when you are facing a storm and your boat gets rocked. There is word-power inside you to rebuke the high waves, wind, and water! God wants to do mighty works and miracles through those with great faith. Will you believe that God has plans for you? It is time to be still and silent in order become wise in your future faith walk.

Still Point Moment

Have you ever been in a situation asking God if He cares what you are going through? If you felt afraid, why did you? If so, be still and understand that God is there. Your faith in God is key to receiving your blessings. God works through your faith. Faith will lead you towards a revelation and understanding of God while you are maturing in Christ. In order for you to gain and receive these promises you must know who God the Father, Jesus the Son, and Holy Spirit as the Comforter are in your life. The Trinity Team is near and on duty. Be still (pray) and silent (listen and look for God) in the storm. Don't lose your faith when your boat is rocked.

Preface Still Point Reflection

God is bigger than your circumstances and problems. So where is your faith? Remember, faith in God will take you to your next level and bring new connections. Jesus told the woman who touched the hem of his robe, *"Daughter, your faith has made you well. Go in peace. You have been healed (Mark 5:34)."* Faith in God will also give you courage to live in your next level, face the next test, and go through your situation. If your boat gets rocked, have faith and speak to the storm! After Jesus calmed the winds and waves, the boat made it to the other side (Mark 5:1). As soon as the boat crossed the lake, Jesus healed a man in the land of the Gerasenes (Mark 5:1-8). The storm could not keep Jesus from reaching this man. God had plans for this man to be healed. Therefore, you have to understand that the adversary wants to rob you from your blessing.

You are on your way to the next level of the Jeremiah 29:11 plans God has for you! Stay in the boat and keep your faith like the disciples. Have courage to rebuke the raging winds and waves that rock your boat. Also, be ready for your instant change once healed and delivered by Jesus. Your faith will become a testimony to tell someone how wonderful and merciful the Lord has been.

Still Transition Affirmation

You can grow spiritually into your Jeremiah 29:11 identity and assignment by understanding how Biblical people prayed, looked to God, and separated themselves from others. God is faithful and will fulfill all His promises to you. You can transition into the plans God has for you with affirmations. All you need to do is make room in your heart and reconnect your spiritual and human beings to the glory and image of God.

Let me encourage you to have hope in God's promises. As you read this book, believe that God is real in your situation. All you need is hope and faith. Discover your Jeremiah 29:11 identity through the connections of the Biblical people who transformed their lives in the faith of Jesus.

Section One. Discovering God's Plans and Path is the designated part for you to acknowledge God as your Heavenly Father and in order to stay on your Jeremiah 29:11 path. You will discover how to stay in the plans God has for you.

Section Two. Discovering God's Wisdom is designed for you to have hope as you read about Biblical women and their victories over obstacles. You will discover how these women had hope that their situations would change.

Section Three. Chosen for Ministry presents the ministry plan God has for you to bless your home, family, and community. This section is written for you to know that you are chosen to do God's will and have an assignment to bless other people.

Section Four. The Ministry of Motherhood reveals the sacrifices Biblical women made when God revealed the gifts and plans God had for their children. This section offers hope for women assigned to children as they encounter challenges and help them to have faith and hope.

SECTION 1: DISCOVERING GOD'S PLANS AND PATH

God's Plans for Women: The Jeremiah 29:11 Plans and Path

Still Point: *Keep steady my steps according to your promise, and let no iniquity have dominion over me (Psalm 119:133).*

The Lord is keeping your feet steady on the Jeremiah 29:11 path. Let this book guide you page by page to the plans God has for you. You will read about Biblical men and women who God used to carry out His plans for the generations. Many of them faced and experienced obstacles (maybe you can relate). The purpose of this design is to identify the essence of the Word of God in the plans for you. As you read, I want to encourage you to make connections and explore your new understanding about God's plan for you. Woman of God, it's time "to go to the altar of God, to God—the source of all my joy (Psalm 43:4)." The plans God has for you are plans to prosper you spiritually. Therefore, I want to encourage you to stay encouraged while you walk into your Jeremiah 29:11 plans. Your path may look like a track course, but let me encourage you to stay in your Jeremiah 29:11 lane. Begin developing your Jeremiah 29:11 identity with these verses from Psalm.

1. *(Psalm 25:4-5) Show me the path where I should walk, O Lord; point out the right road for me to follow (4). Lead me by your truth and teach me, for you are the God who saves me. All day long I put hope in you (5).*

2. *(Psalm 119:133) Keep steady my steps according to your promise, and let no iniquity have dominion over me.*

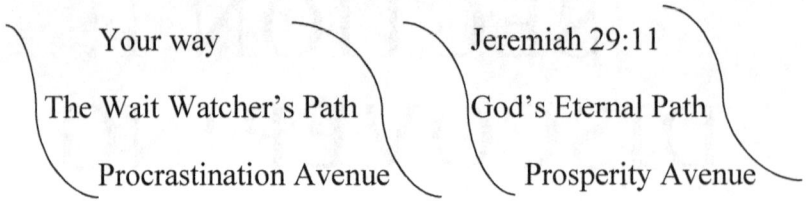

Your way

The Wait Watcher's Path

Procrastination Avenue

Jeremiah 29:11

God's Eternal Path

Prosperity Avenue

My sister, I want to encourage you not to choose the "Wait Watcher's Path." A woman in, "The Wait Watcher's Path," is an individual who can visualize their destiny and not take the necessary steps to their vision. People in the "Wait Watchers Path," destroy their vision with their excuses and heavy feet. Did you know that excuses can cause a pattern and lifestyle in your life that yields empty results?

Excuses in the mind and out of a person's mouth can put a halt in their reach and make their feet stuck. Also, excuses in the mind are signs of unbelief. Unbelief can hinder your relationship with God. God wants you to reach out your arms to Him through a relationship. You need your mind free of excuses to have faith to reach and step into your goals. A mind freed from excuses can see and execute the vision. To avoid heavy feet you have to walk by faith (II Corinthians 5:7). Command your Jeremiah 29:11 vision to come to pass, and stretch into it the vision with faith.

Execute the Vision

Execution of the vision will win every time when obstacles come in your path. Let me encourage you that *now* is the time for you to execute what you visualize through planning. Planning ahead helps to give you direction when deciding what path to take. Your only direction for achieving your Jeremiah 29:11 identity is to take God's Eternal Path. However, if you take the "Wait Watcher's Path," you're procrastinating. Procrastination Avenue only leads a person to make excuses and become stuck with unfinished tasks. Some people wait for the conditions to get better and they ignore their self-discovery and calling. For some women, facing the facts requires separation and space from people and places; and for others it's waiting for perfect conditions. Examine your situation honestly and have faith the size of a mustard seed to step out into the Jeremiah 29:11 purpose for you.

Use Solomon's wisdom in Ecclesiastes 14:4 to guide your self-evaluation. *Ecclesiastes 11:4, "If you wait for perfect conditions, you will never get anything done."* It is important to manage and organize your external factors and make room in your heart to execute the vision and make the command. Let me encourage you to face and examine your situations. While facing your issues, you may need to separate from some people and places and create space within your home to grow and to develop your talents. Facing *your* facts involves recognizing your external and internal conditions. Your present condition is part of the process to your destiny. Does your condition align with the Word of God?

Take a moment to evaluate your path. Don't allow your feet to get heavy with a pattern of excuses and procrastination. Are you wondering, "How did I get here?" or "When is this going to be over?" Your Jeremiah 29:11 path will lead you into self-discovery. In this process, you will face the facts that you had to race or run, walk, stand still, jump, cry, smile, rejoice, give birth, experience lost, grieve, or learn to wait for something in your season of self-discovery. Let me encourage you to take God's eternal path which can lead to a discovery of your Jeremiah 29:11 identities. Begin to write out your goals and make short and long-term goals to execute your vision. Continue to execute your vision when obstacles arise.

Command the vision

You have gifts and talents to help others and yourself in discovering their Jeremiah 29:11 identities. Your self-discovery will lead others into discovering their spirituality, develop career awareness, skills and interests, gifts, and talents. Therefore, you cannot faint or get tired this season. Let me encourage you to execute your vision by making a command. Solomon explains this in Ecclesiastes 9:11:

"I have observed something else in this world of ours. The fastest runner doesn't always win the race, and the strongest warrior doesn't always win the battle. The wise are often poor, and the skillful are not necessarily wealthy. And those who are educated don't always

lead successful lives. It is all decided by chance, by being at the right place at the right time."

You cannot lose. Let me encourage you to focus on your vision when challenges arise because you have a Jeremiah 29:11 identity. You are at the right place at the right time designed by the Jeremiah 29:11 plan for you to live victoriously and triumph over the hurdles in the path that's designed for you. Jeremiah 29:11 identifies that God has plans for you, and this means that you have to let go of fear while you are on this treasure hunt. Trust in God in all you do. You are at the starting line of your treasure hunt. Begin to start taking command of the things in your life. You have been tolerating things (e.g. your situation) too long! It's time for a change. The command of this scripture is to speak to it! If there is a mountain in your Jeremiah 29:11 plan, the action here is to identify the mountain (your struggle) and speak to it in order to change it. Also, this self-discovery will develop your ability to operate in joy according to James 1:3-6 when obstacles try to discourage you.

James 1:(3) "For when your faith is tested, your endurance has a chance to grow. (4) So let it grow, for when your endurance is fully developed, you will be strong in character and ready for anything. (5) If you need wisdom-if you want to know what God wants you to do-ask Him, and He will gladly tell you. He will not resent your asking. (6) But when you ask Him, be sure that you really expect him to answer, for a doubtful mind is as unsettled as a wave of the sea that is driven and tossed by the wind"

I want to encourage you to walk in the Jeremiah 29:11 plans. Being conscious of the scriptures is the beginning of a strong faith and victorious walk. Be conscious of how to tolerate, accept, endure, and withstand in your self-discovery. Ask God for wisdom to identify people's motives and plans for you. God will order your steps with grace towards victory! Runners expect victory at the finish line, but conquers seek after the victory before the race! Fighters step into the match as winners! Walk in the Jeremiah 29:11 plans with victory to conquer like the Biblical men and women presented in this book.

So far, you've learned page by page how to execute the vision, command the vision, run, and fight! God will give you grace as you continue to walk in your Jeremiah 29:11 plans. Grace covers your life and gives strength for your faith walk. You have been ordained and graced for the Jeremiah 29:11 identity, purpose, and plans for you. Expect victory as God gives you grace in your lane!

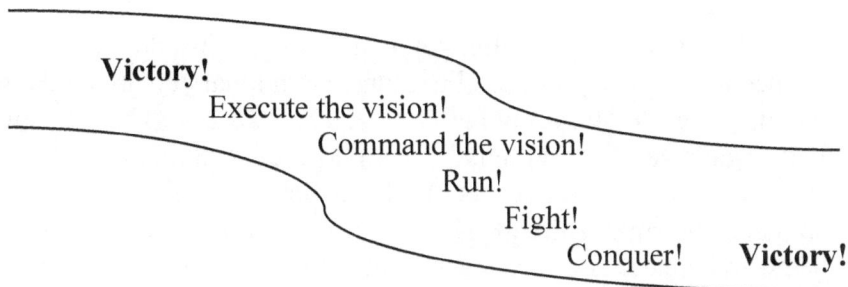

Victory!
Execute the vision!
Command the vision!
Run!
Fight!
Conquer!   **Victory!**

Stretch for the Unreachable

You were created on purpose, for God's purpose:

"For I know the plans I have for you," declares the Lord, "plans to prosper you and not to harm you, plans to give you hope and a future." (Jeremiah 29:11).

Women of God, our Heavenly Father has created, shaped, formed, and designed you as a vessel to nurture life. You were created to give birth, grow, and nurture beings; teach the principles of the laws to children; and train children to give honor to their elders. Most of all you are created to minister the Word of God to your children. The responsibilities and purposes of Women of God are to sow the Word of God into our children in order to make them fruitful and knowledgeable in spiritual ways. We are also responsible for training them in the way to go (Proverbs 22:6).

Understand that you possess victory in your walk and talk! For these reasons, you have to execute and command your vision. Begin to thank God for the victories He has already won for you. Believe it! You are queens, overcomers, conquerors, and winners of every situation because of your daily faith.

You are a Light

In the beginning the Word already existed He was with God, and He was God (John 1:1). (2) He was in the beginning with God. (3) He created everything there is. Nothing exists that he didn't make. (4) Life itself was in Him, and this life gives light to everyone.

There is a light within you that gives you insight and connection to your purpose. First, understand that you are made in the image of our Heavenly Father (Genesis 1:26-27). The Heavenly Father gave you life and light. Your purpose is within this light. Your purpose is to be masters of all life, fish, birds, livestock, wild animals, and small animals. This means you have the authority to name and create. You are made in the image of God. Therefore you have the ability to speak those things that are not as though they were. You have a faith walk and talk that sustain you when challenges arise. Therefore, you should keep your eyes on the vision and trust in the plans God has given you.

Secondly, you were made to respond to God's word in the Jeremiah 29:11 plans for you. You become a Daughter of God once you realize that you have a purpose in the Kingdom. Therefore, you have to perceive that your children, those you are assigned to teach, and people you interact with have a Jeremiah 29:11 identity and purpose. You have a responsibility to search out and understand these plans for you and the people you are assigned to through a relationship with God.

Step in with Faith

God is our Father, and we are created in His image. We are his sons and daughters in the kingdom. The purpose of sons and daughters of God is Kingdom building with people on Earth as it is in Heaven. First, you have to accept His engagement. God is asking us, "Will you marry me?" Will you marry His will and seek Him? Will you trust Him and allow Him to bless you? Second, will you acknowledge His love and accept His engagement and commit to His kingdom? He gave His only Son so that you will not perish but live with Him in the Kingdom. Will you marry Him? After accepting His engagement, you'll become His sons and daughters. Will you accept His engagement?

You are moving along, page by page, to discover the plans God has for you. Let me encourage you to stay in the plans God has for you to leap over any hurdles along the way. Believe that you have a light within you to stretch, walk, visualize, and step in the plans and promises God has for you.

Treasure my Instruction

You were made in the image of God and that makes you His daughter. Therefore, you have a Jeremiah 29:11 identity that you need to discover. There are promises in the plans for you to have hope and prosper in your day-to-day life. These promises are tied to seeds in the people and places you will meet and interact with throughout the seasons of your life created by our Heavenly Father. It's important for you to have a relationship with God in order to recognize these promises and His plan. In the Word of God, the Lord details the course of action you must take in order to become wise.

The first step necessary in this pursuit is learning to fear the Lord. Proverbs 1:7 states, *"Fear of the Lord is the beginning of knowledge, but only fools despise wisdom and discipline."* A key aspect of fearing God is developing the ability to listen both to God and to the wise counsel sent by God to bless you into your purpose. Proverbs 1:5 says, *"Let the wise listen and add to their learning."* Listening is the next key to understanding the Jeremiah 29:11 plans and identity.

Proverbs 2:1 My children listen to me and treasure my instruction. (2) Tune your ears to wisdom, and concentrate on understanding. (3) Cry out for insight and understanding. (4) Search for them as you would for lost money or hidden treasure. (5) Then you will understand what it means to fear the Lord, and you will gain knowledge of God. (6) For the Lord grants wisdom! From his mouth come knowledge and understanding. (7) He grants a treasure of good sense to the godly. He is their shield, protecting those who walk with integrity. (8) He guards the paths of justice and protects those who are faithful to him. (9) Then you will understand what is right, just, and fair, and you will know how to find the right course of action every time. (10) For wisdom will enter your heart, and knowledge

will fill you with joy. (11) Wise planning will watch over you.
Understanding will keep you safe.

The reward for seeking God's wisdom and insight with new understanding comes after you have searched and found the Father. His rewards come in all shapes and sizes from good sense to the godly, and they are a shield to protect those who walk with integrity. As you listen to God, meditate on the Word day and night. God guards the paths and protects those who are faithful to Him. God's wisdom and his commandments enter your heart and fill you with joy.

(Proverbs 3:1) My child, never forget the things I have taught you. Store my commandments in your heart. (2) For they will give you a long and satisfying life. (3) Never let loyalty and kindness get away from you! Wear them like a necklace; write them deep within your heart, (4) Then you will find favor with both God and people, and you will find favor with both God and people, and you will gain a good reputation. (5) Trust in the Lord with all your heart; do not depend on your own understanding. (6) Seek His will in all that you do, and He will direct your paths. (7) Don't be impressed with your own wisdom. Instead, fear the Lord and turn your back on evil. (8) Then you will gain renewed health and vitality.

You have a responsibility to listen and understand the Jeremiah 29:11 plans and identity God has for you. Are you accepting your role as you continue to discover treasure? God has a plan and purpose for your life and you have to seek Him. God provided you with wisdom and commandments to apply to your daily walk and talk. These commandments remind us to fear God, be obedient, and establish a covenant with Him. It's important to trust God and make Him the head of your life. You can depend on God to work out every situation in your life because He paved the way for you. God speaks His wisdom to us in His Word which is why you have to, *"trust in the Lord with all your heart; do not depend on your own understanding (Proverbs 3:5)."*

There are many benefits when you put God first and trust His commandments (Psalms 103). The benefits include gains such as a renewed health and vitality (Proverbs 3:8), favor with both God and people, and a good reputation (Proverb 3:8). It is in our best interest to develop an intimate relationship with God. So far you have been introduced to treasuring the plans God has for you in your heart with wisdom and to a relationship with our Creator. Be encouraged as you continue in your Jeremiah 29:11 plans.

Today, you have become engaged to Him and now have a Kingdom purpose to discover. You were created to complete Kingdom plans and purpose. You were created by His Word and made in His image to complete His plans. What are the plans God has for you? Throughout this book, you will journey to discover His plans for you. During this journey, you will become a witness as you experience God's love for you. He created you on purpose with a purpose. You will discover that He loves you and has saved you from weapons that were formed against you. *Jeremiah 29:11 The Plans I Have for You: Woman, Walk in Victory* will guide you to discover the treasures and gifts in your purpose.

Have you discovered the light you hold? *"But this precious treasure, this light and power that now shines within us is held in perishable containers, that is, in our weak bodies. So everyone can see that our glorious power is from God and is not our own…" II Corinthians 4:7.* To begin this treasure hunt, you have to stay on the path of righteousness, seek wisdom, have faith, and develop your relationship with God. After seeking God, you will find your treasures (Hebrew 11:6), and you will continue to see situations differently.

Your future is waiting on your strategy as you begin your treasure hunt to discover the Jeremiah 29:11 plans and purposes. It's time for you to step into and start walking in your Jeremiah 29:11 path. This book will guide you in discovering your Jeremiah 29:11 identity, planting good seeds into your ground, and working in the reaped harvest that has been promised to you. As you prepare this new quest, make sure the lights are on. How do you turn on the lights? You have to let God's Word be a lamp for your feet and a light for your path (Psalm 119:105). I pray that you gain an overflowing spiritual and fruitful vocabulary as you journey and study mighty Biblical women of God. Your Jeremiah 29:11 path includes an identity, plan, purpose, and promise spoken by God before you were born. Be encouraged as you continue to read page-by-page how Biblical characters discovered and stayed on their Jeremiah purpose.

Continue to walk in the Jeremiah 29:11 path for you. Make room in your heart to receive and understand your purpose. Let me encourage you to have hope in your situation no matter how hard it may seem. God has already destined for you to have victory in your situation. Therefore, you have to remain aligned with the Jeremiah 29:11 plans with hope in the Lord. Write down your goals and strategize how you plan to accomplish those plans with yourself, family, house, career, and education. Don't worry if your plans and goals get interrupted. This may be God orchestrating Heaven's benefits to meet your needs to your goal. This means that you have to have hope that God is working out everything to meet your Jeremiah 29:11 identity.

Still Point Moment: What are your goals? How do your goals match your mission? What actions are you making to fulfill your goals? Are your talents and gifts related to your goals? Stay on the Jeremiah 29:11 path to discover God's plans for you according to His purpose.

Still Transition Affirmation: I have hope in the Lord. *My only hope is in your unfailing love and faithfulness (Psalm 40: 11b).*

God's Plan for Women: How to stay in the Plans God has for You

Still Point: *(Psalms 25:4) Show me the path where I should walk, O Lord; point out the right road for me to follow. (5) Lead me by your truth and teach me, for you are the God who saves me. All day long I put my hope in you.*

God is showing you which path to walk. Now that you are on the path God designed for you, it is important to learn how to recognize and overcome obstacles. This section is designed to guide you in discovering your purpose. Have you ever wondered where your purpose began? Let me explain to you how God planted a purpose in you before you were conceived in your mother's womb.

In His goodness He chose to make us His own children by giving us His true word. And we, out of all creation, became His choice possession (James 1:18).

Adam was spoken of before he was created (Genesis 1:26). Your purpose was formed in God's womb and planted in the womb of your mother. Yes, you were created (Genesis 1:26) from the beginning (Genesis 1:1 & 1:26) with Jeremiah 29:11 plans and purpose for your life and fabricated by God's design, divinity, and direction.

It's time to be followers of the Will of God. In Matthew 6:33, it tells us to *"Seek ye first the kingdom of God, and all these things will be added to you."* What things will be added? First, God will provide when you seek Him to develop your purpose. Second, there are awards when you seek God. Third, there are blessings when you ask for them.

Your purpose in life is to give God glory and build His Kingdom. Your first step in self-discovery begins with you accepting Jesus Christ as your Savior. This step is important in discovering God's plans for you. The following steps help you to strategize how to align your body to follow your mind and spirit:

Step One: Accept Jesus Christ as your Lord and Savior.

Step Two: Prepare your bodies for this treasure hunt by surrendering all to God. Forgive those who have trespassed against you. Alter your thinking and give negative thoughts and experiences to God. If you need further assistance, write out these experiences, names, and incidents that hurt and hindered your thinking. Pray over your list and then rip it up.

Step Three: Prepare your bodies for consecration. It's your time to breakout so that God can break through because God is a master mender and healer of broken pieces. Let me encourage you to give it to God. Today, declare that you are coming out of your wilderness and into the will of God. Consecrate yourself, lean on the Lord, and seek His kingdom and righteousness.

Step Four: As you begin this treasure pursuit, you have to invite the Holy Spirit to dwell in your body. You start this process by understanding that your body is God's Temple.

(1 Corinthians 6:19) that your body is the temple of the Holy Spirit, who lives in you and was given to you by God? You do not belong to yourself, (20) for God brought you with a high price. So you must honor God with your body.

Make room in your heart by moving out the mess created by negative thinking, unforgiveness, and experiences. God can work through you with a clean heart and right spirit. You can invite the Holy Spirit to engage and guide you into your purpose once you clear out and let go of the hurt. Begin to encourage yourself with your treasure search.

Step Five: You have to know that God created you with a spiritual package complete with gifts and talents. This package was created and spoke of in the beginning according to John 1:1. God revealed to Jeremiah that He formed, set apart, and appointed him with an assignment.

Jeremiah 1:5, "I knew you before I formed you in your mother's womb. Before you were born I set you apart and appointed you as my spokesman to the world."

God is speaking to the Prophet Jeremiah about the Genesis 1:26 package and purpose for the Israelites. Again, God has mapped out your purpose and given you the keys and words to speak and unlock your heavenly treasures.

Jeremiah 1:9 says, Then the Lord touched my mouth and said, "See, I have put my words in your mouth!" Woman of God, you have a Jeremiah message. The Word says in *Matthew 17:20 "even if you have faith as small as a mustard seed you could say to this mountain, 'Move from here to there,' and it will move. Nothing would be impossible."*

Having faith is a key component to receiving your treasure. The strategy to begin power talk begins with applying the fruit of the Spirit into your walk. You will have to spend time with God as you continue to walk in your Jeremiah 29:11 path. This means that you have to discover the Jeremiah 29:11 seed that is planted in you. Place faith as your first destination in discovering the rewards on your map.

Step Six: Have a revelation. Now that faith is on your map, you can begin seeking God and receive your treasures. You have to proceed in the desire to know Jesus. How do you declare and identify Jesus? In Matthew 16:15, Jesus asks the disciples,

"Who do you say I am?" In verse (16), Simon Peter answered, "You are the Messiah, the Son of the living God." (17) Jesus replied, "You are blessed, Simon son of John, because my Father in heaven has revealed this to you. You did not learn this from any human being. (18) Now I say to you that you are Peter, and upon this rock I will build my church, and all the powers of hell will not conquer it."

Amen! This scripture is to encourage you to know that God will give you revelation. God can be revealed in a revelation. God will be revealed when you recognize His works just like Simon Peter. Revelation is a spiritual awareness of Kingdom secrets that help you become a manager of the plans God has for you.

"Now, a person who is put in charge as a manager must be faithful (I Corinthians 4:2)."

In the Jeremiah 29:11 plans God has for you, it is important to manage your mind, body, soul, and time. Your faith is going to be tested; therefore it is important to have balance in your life when trials and obstacles come about. Remember these steps as you continue to manage your life, home, and children. The Jeremiah 29:11 plans God has for you are mapped out with divine miracles, signs, and wonders. These elements are keys to reveal God in your life and add to your faith. There are no "powers of hell" nor weapon formed to alter the revelation that God has given you to complete your Jeremiah 29:11 purposes.

Matthew 16:19, "And I will give you the keys of the Kingdom of Heaven. Whatever you lock on earth will be locked in Heaven, and whatever you open on earth will be opened in heaven."

Take your keys! You have doors to open! God has prepared your access and opened the door for you to experience hope in your prosperous future according to Jeremiah 29:11. You have the keys to your breakthrough, which means you are managers for your prosperity. The following scriptures can encourage you to believe in your purpose.

1. *Jude 1:20 But you, dear friends, must continue to build your lives on the foundation of your holy faith. And continue to pray as you are directed by the Holy Spirit. (21) Live in such a way that God's love can bless you as you wait for the eternal life that our Lord Jesus Christ in His mercy is going to give you.*

2. *Romans 12:2, Don't copy the behavior and customs of this world, but let God transform you into a new person by changing the way you think. Then you will know what God wants you to do, and you will know how well and lasting the perfect His Will really is.*

God does not want us to be like the heirs of the world. For what profits you to gain the world and lose your soul? What do you gain from sinning? Walk in your Jeremiah 29:11 Path. You will lose old habits and gain fruitful actions to succeed while you begin seeking your reward and finding your treasure. Get ready to take on a new talk and walk. Begin to pray daily, and worship and praise God throughout the day as you develop into your purpose. The Lord knows what you need before you ask. When you pray, go into a room and pray to the Heavenly Father in secret; and He sees in secret and will reward you.

The Lord's Prayer can help you to pray and reveal the Heavenly Father. Jesus introduced this prayer in His ministry. Let me encourage you to recite this prayer daily in your life and teach it to your children and others.

1. **Prayer: Matthew 6:8-13** *Matthew 6:8 Don't be like them because your Father knows exactly what you need even before you ask Him! (9) Pray like this, "Our Father in Heaven, may your name be honored. May your Kingdom come soon. (10) May your will be done here on earth, just as it is in Heaven. (11) Give us food for today, (12) and forgive us our sins, just as we have forgiven those who have sinned against us. (13) And don't let us yield to temptation, but deliver us from the evil one.*

2. **Prayer: Luke 11:1-4.** *Luke 11:1 Once when Jesus had been out praying, one of his disciples came to him as he finished and said, "Lord, teach us to pray, just as John taught his disciples." (2) He said, "This is how you should pray: "Father, may your name be honored. May you Kingdom come soon. (3) Give us our food day by day. (4) And forgive us our sins-just as we forgive those who have sinned against us. And don't let us yield to temptation.*

As you follow God, on your path you will find treasures in the shadow of the Almighty if you choose to live in its shelter (Psalms 91:1). The Lord is your refuge and place of safety; and you have to trust God while in His shadow. If you find that your thoughts wondered in *the dark valley of death (Psalm 23:4),* do not be afraid. God will rescue you from every trap and protect you from fatal plague.

He will shield you with His wings. He will shelter you with His feathers. His faithful promises are your armor and protection (Psalm 91:2-4).

I'm encouraging you to walk in the Jeremiah 29:11 Path that God has purposely made for you. If you feel discouraged or your thoughts wondered in *the dark valley*, dance and rejoice in the Lord anyhow. Build a mindset that is geared to fully rely on God and follow Him. Speak, *'Let there be light!'* in every situation and conversation with people. Faith is your key to get you started for your destiny and to lead you towards your destination. Your faith is the key to open and close doors. Prayer will give you strength to continue in purpose.

Jeremiah 29:11 Path:
God planted me in my purpose
I was created on purpose
I accept my engagement to the Word of God
I will step into God's Will

Step into God's Will

Jesus has given you the keys and it's in your hands to unlock your treasures. First, you have to start with faith; and by believing and not by seeing (II Corinthians 5:7). Second, you need to have a desire to know your purpose and the plans God has for you. This begins by sowing the Word of God in your heart and speaking it out of your mouth to pray, move mountains, and unlock your treasures. Next, make room to receive more word, revelation, strength, and power while continuing on your treasure quest. As you begin to seek God, He will renew the way you think along the path for, *"Great is His faithfulness; His mercies begins afresh each day"* (Lamentations 3:23). Questions and answers will surface as you unlock and lock doors to your season.

Now as you begin your journey, you are going to have to pack some fruit to eat along the way. Let's go visit the storehouse, and get some fruit because you are going to need it along the way. Most of all, you are going to need spiritual covering, guidance, and comfort directing you towards your treasure. I'm talking about the Holy Spirit.

Galatians 5:22-23, "But when the Holy Spirit controls our lives, he will produce this kind of fruit in us: love, joy, peace, patience, kindness, goodness, faithfulness, gentleness, and self-control. Here there is no conflict."

Applying these fruits into our daily lives requires submission to pray, study, fast, worship to walk according to the fruits of the spirit. You have to develop Fruit Actions to get full of the Spirit. *"Though our bodies are dying, our spirits are being renewed every day" (II Corinthians 4:16).* While your journey is beginning, you are going to need renewal daily. You will need this daily renewal to recognize your path and the people you meet along the way. Meaning, you need to have the fruits of the spirit to identify the motives and intentions other people are trying to serve or produced (Luke 6:43), especially if they are in your path. What fruits have you picked up from others? Who gave you some bad fruit? What does your fruit look like? Is your fruit rotten or ripped?

It's time to pray and walk on the right path because the Jeremiah 29:11 seed within you needs to grow. Your gifts and talents are designed to build the Kingdom of God on Earth and bless others. Therefore, it is important to have faith in order to develop the fruits of spirit into fruit actions according to Galatians 5:22-23! As you continue to discover your purpose (your light) and you become thirsty or hungry follow the guide below:

1. **Drink from Heaven's fountain.** *John 7:37, "If you are thirsty, come to me! (38) If you believe in me, come and drink! For the Scriptures declare that rivers of living water will flow out from within."*
2. **Eat His bread.** *John 6:48, "Yes, I am the bread of life (50) However, the bread from heaven gives eternal life to everyone who eats it. (51) I am the living bread that came down out of heaven.*
3. **Trust and believe.** *Isaiah 41:10 "Don't be afraid, for I am with you. Do not be dismayed for I am your God. I will strengthen you. I will help you. I will uphold you with my victorious hand. (11) See, all your enemies lie there, confused and ashamed. Anyone who opposes you will die. (12) You will*

look for them in vain. They will be gone. (13) I am holding you by your right hand, I the Lord your God. And I say to you "Do not be afraid. I am here to help you."

Pack your water to drink as you journey to your purpose to discover your treasures. Along the way, don't faint if you feel weak. The Lord will supply your needs and give you strength to complete your Jeremiah 29:11 assignments.

Still Point Moments: Drink, eat, and build a relationship with the Lord. Have faith in the plans God has for you. God will work through your faith. Let me encourage you to have big faith this season as you walk on you Jeremiah 29:11 Path.

Still Affirmation: I will wait and trust in the Lord. *"But those who wait on the Lord will find new strength. They will fly high on wings like eagles. They will run and not grow weary, they will walk and not faint (Isaiah 40:31)."*

God's Plan for Women: Let Go!

Still Point: I cry out to the Lord; I plead for the Lord's mercy. I pour out my complaints before Him and tell Him all my troubles. For I am overwhelmed, and you alone know the way I should turn (Psalm 142:1-3).

The Lord knows the way you should turn. You can't faint in this season! God has given you grace to stay strong this season. You have to recognize Jesus when He is talking to you. During this treasure hunt your worship will develop and you will recognize how Jesus has been in your path blessing you. He has supplied all your needs and kept the water in your well during your seasons. The prophecy God spoken over your life has been strategically designed for you. Therefore, you can overcome obstacles and cannot remain the way that you are! GOD HAS PLANS FOR YOU!

Believe and conceive that you are more than a conqueror according to Romans 8: 17. Believe and conceive that you are complete in Him according to Colossians 2:10. Also, believe and conceive that you are redeemed according to Galatians 3:13. Get to know God in a personal way. Jesus came so that each of us could know and understand God in a personal way. Knowing Jesus can bring meaning and purpose to life.

John 3:16 For God so loved the world that He gave His only begotten Son that whosoever believes in Him should not perish but have everlasting life. (17) For God did not send his Son into the world to condemn the world, but to save the world through Him.
(Galatians 5:16) We have the present help of the Holy Spirit to cover us in our walk with God. But I say, walk by the Spirit, and you will not gratify the desires of the flesh.

There is a plan and purpose for you. Let me encourage you to walk and talk with God to discover the plans and purposes for you. Prayer time with God is key to stay on your Jeremiah 29:11 Path. Woman of God, you must walk by faith and not by sight (II Cor 1:7). Begin to pray and ask God for the wisdom to access and accomplish the plans God has for you and your children. As a mother, there is a time when you must push your children into their purpose. There is a time to train and let go, as Mary did for Jesus (John 2: 1- 12). Mary believed in Jesus because she had a revelation from the angel, and knew his purpose. Remember, you are protected as you walk in your purpose. Walk in victory with a let-go attitude rather than a moody conditional attitude so the fruits of the spirit can grow and operate your purpose. May you discover your Jeremiah 29:11 purpose with hope, pray, and know that the presence of God is on you. Believe and conceive what you need with faith. God is providing the things you need along this journey. You have what it takes to complete what you believe and conceived according to God.

Still Point Moment: Stay strong in the plans God has for you. Make room in your heart to receive Heavenly benefits needed to accomplish the goals and strategies to build yourself, home, children, husband, and career and education.

Still Transition Affirmation: I will stay on the Jeremiah 29:11 Path. *Travel steadily along his path (Psalm 37:34b).*

God's Plans for Woman: Understand your Gifts

Still Point: *For the Lord watches over the path of the godly, but the path of the wicked leads to destruction (Psalm 1:6).*

God is watching over your path. *(Genesis 1:26-28) Then God said, "Let us make people in our image to be like ourselves. They will be masters over all life-the fish in the sea, the birds in the sky, and all the livestock, wild animals, and small animals. (27) So God created people in His own image; God patterned them after himself; male and female He created them. (28) God blessed them and told them, "Multiply and fill the earth and subdue it. Be masters over the fish and birds and all the animals."*

These scriptures give us revelation that God created us in the beginning on the sixth day and tagged us with Jeremiah 29:11 plans to prosper and live. God created us in the beginning on the sixth day according to Genesis. You were given a Jeremiah 29:11 identity and purpose, which is the gift of life when God breathe in to you. You were made with purpose and given an assignment according to Jeremiah 1:5. God told Jeremiah that He knew him before he was conceived in the womb. Meaning that:

We are spiritual: From His breath, He gave us purpose!

We are a spoken Word: From His mouth, we are a delivered Word!

We are an existing Word from the Spirit of His womb: From His mouth and by His Word, we were born!

We were formed and shaped in the palm of His hands: We are from our Father.

Gifts in God's Image

Not only are you made in God's image, you also have His gifts and talents. That's why it is important to walk by faith and conceive the image of God. God has given you grace according to the measure of the gift of Christ (Ephesians 4:7). There is a prophecy spoken over your life and you have dominion and power to prosper.

Just as God made Heaven and Earth, the purpose for Heaven and Earth is to supply our needs to complete Kingdom purpose. Every mountain, valley, river, ocean, state, city, and land has a purpose to meet your need. God spoke these things into existence to meet our needs and purpose. God formed man into His image and breathe life into the form. God formed and made man and woman with gifts to use according to His purpose. All gifts are connected and come from God.

Let's examine scriptures that explain the ministries of the body of the church so you can discover your Jeremiah 29:11 plans and purpose.

Ephesians 4:11, He is the one who gave these gifts to the church: the apostles, the prophets, the evangelists, and the pastors and teachers, (12) There responsibility is to equip God's people to do His work and build up the church, the body of Christ, (13) until we come to such unity in our faith and knowledge of God's Son that we will be mature and full grown in the Lord, measuring up to the full stature of Christ.
Romans 12:6, God has given each of us the ability to do certain things well. So if God has given you the ability to prophesy, speak out when you have faith that God is speaking through you. (7) If your gift is that of serving others, serve them well. If you are a teacher, do a good job of teaching. (8) If your gift is to encourage others, do it! If you have money, share it generously. If God has given you leadership ability, take the responsibility seriously. And if you have a gift of showing kindness to others, do it gladly! (11) Never be lazy in your work, but serve the Lord enthusiastically.

Woman of God, you have these gifts to face any obstacle! You have a Jeremiah 29:11 seed to do things well. You are designed to be a builder, creator, and giver. You are raising sons and daughters with precious spiritual gifts, and we have to read the Word of God and hear from God to train up our children. You have the ability to build and transform your life to align to the Jeremiah 29:11 plans for you. Most of all, you have to be connected to those who believe in the Word and recognize God in the mist. Your Jeremiah 29:11 plans and purposes are designed to build the Kingdom of God and God's people. Therefore, it is important for you to operate in the Galatians 5:22-23 fruits of the Spirit to meet the needs or make exchanges with the people of God.

Still Point Moment: The gift of grace is for you to be strong when facing obstacles. Let me encourage you to face each situation with the victory concept. This means that you will walk in victory in your Jeremiah 29:11 Path. Do not limit God or give up early because grace is always leading you toward victory

Still Transition Affirmation: God loves me. *For God so loved the world, that he gave his only Son, so that everyone who believes in him would not perish, but have eternal life (John 3:16).*

You can transform your life to align to the plans God has for you. Your gifts and talents depend on your heart to be right and in order to operate in the plans God has for you.

God's Plan for Women: Connect to Your Senses

Still Point: *I will bless the Lord who guides me; even at night my heart instructs me. I know the Lord is always with me (Psalm 16:7). (8) I will not be shaken, for he is right beside me (8).*

The Lord is guiding you and instructing your heart. How do you know when God is speaking? God will speak to your heart when your heart belongs to Him. You are gifted, talented, and wonderfully made (Psalm 139:14) by the Heavenly Creator. This means that your life and body need to be aligned with God's plans for you. You have to live holy and right.

Let them be a living and holy sacrifice, the kind he will accept (Romans 12:1). (2) Don't copy the behavior and customs of this world, but let God transform you in a new person by changing the way you think.

God's grace is upon you to complete your Jeremiah assignment. Woman of God, use all your five senses to build yourself and home, and train and prepare your child for Kingdom building; which means you have to guard what you see, hear, taste, feel, and say. You can transform into a new person through your five senses. These five senses are doors to your spirit.

Keep your eyes on the Lord. *Your eyes are always looking to the Lord for help, for he alone can rescue me from the traps of my enemies (Psalms 25:15).*

Keep your ears listening to the Lord. Your ears are listening to the message of the Good News about Christ; faith comes by hearing (Romans 10:17).

Taste and see that the Lord is good. Your taste for the Word of God will increase as you continue to seek and chase after Him. God's favor has flavor. God will use you to be a blessing to someone else. Your obedience as the blesser will draw that person closer to God.

Your tongue is a sword. The tongue of the wise commends knowledge, but the mouth of the fool gushes folly (Proverbs 15:2). Learn and study the Word of God to bless your life and others. Life and death is in your mouth! Woman of God, it's time to speak life to the Jeremiah 29:11 seeds that are in our children, spouse, and other people assigned to minister and encourage.

The tongue that brings healing is a tree of life but a deceitful tongue crushes the spirit (Proverbs 15:4). The Holy Spirit dwells in the presence and word of God. Read, study, and speak the word of God. Meditate in the word day and night.

Use your **mouth** to speak and confess that you are saved (Romans 10:10).

Touch: *"And there was a woman in the crowd who had a hemorrhage for twelve years. She had spent everything she had on doctors and still could find no cure (Luke 8:43). (44) She came up behind Jesus and touched the fringe of his robe. Immediately, the bleeding stopped."*

Your **hands** will be raised for praise and ready for service. The wealth of the wise is their crown, but the folly of fools yields folly (Proverbs 14:24).

Connecting to your senses will produce fruit actions. Your fruit actions will reflect in praying, fasting, and meditating on the Word of God in the following scriptures:

Pray: *Ephesians 6:1, "In every battle you will need faith as your shield to stop the fiery arrows aimed at you by Satan.*

Ephesians 6:(17) Put on salvation as your helmet, and take the sword of the Spirit, which is word of God. (18) Pray at all times and on every occasion in the power of the Holy Spirit. Stay alert and be persistent in your prayers for all Christians everywhere.

Fast: Present your bodies a living sacrifice. Together, as a body this journey can be easy as we bless one another with our gifts. Your purpose and gifts are to move the Kingdom on Earth as it is in Heaven. Jesus is coming back for the church, His Kingdom!

Mind: Meditate on the Word of God day and night.

Woman of God, you are God's reporter of His goodness and mercy! You are a walking testimony of God's favor! Tell somebody about Jesus and cheer them on, encourage them, and lift them up until they reach their next level.

You will connect your gifts to people as you continue to walk in your Jeremiah 29:11 Path and Plan; however, you have to evaluate their motives. Use your senses to discern those who wants to add to your success and not rob you from the things you've accomplished. You need to know who are the mission carriers and followers of God and those who are pirates.

Pirates will be used as a metaphor to illustrate the people with missions to interrupt and take from you. Pirates are individuals that invade territory that does not belong to them. They operate with the intentions to steal, kill, and destroy (John 10:10). These people are either male or female that come to illegally take your belt or what you hold and invade your property. Therefore, it is important for you to recognize and discern the operations of the people in your crowd that operate like pirates. You have a purpose to complete Kingdom assignments, however remember there will be people operating against your faith, vision, and plans.

As you pursue your treasure (the promise of God), evaluate the people around you. Are your followers crowning or crowding you? Your crowd has a front row seat watching to see are you're going to succeed or give up. Learn to trust God and lean not to your own understanding and in all your ways acknowledge Him (Proverbs 3:5). Let God direct your paths. Let's evaluate your crowd so you can recognize those individuals who pray, support, and add into your purpose.

First, Psalm 1 illustrates how to identify wise persons.

Psalm 1:1 Oh, the joys of those who do not follow the advice of the wicked, or stand around with sinners, or join in with scoffers. (2) But they delight in doing everything the Lord wants; day and night they think about his law. (3) They are like trees planted along the riverbank, bearing fruit each season without fail. Their leaves never whither, and in all they prosper.

You need friends who are counselors, wise, delighters, and commonality interest. Surround yourself with friends or schedule an appointment with people with the Psalm 1:1 gifts and wisdom to add to your assignment.

Counselors will listen to your goals.

Wise persons will pray for you.

Delighters will support your natural strengthens and help build-up weak skills.

Friends/People of commonality will encourage, motivate, and help develop your creativity.

This is important because Satan desires to shake up your life with obstacles, but the Lord has already prayed for you. Yes, God has already prayed for you to have the victory in every situation. Let's look at Luke 22:31-32 when Jesus explains to Simon the plan of the devil:

Luke 22:31, Simon, Simon, Satan has asked to have all of you, to sift you like wheat. (32) But I have pleaded in prayer for you, Simon, that you faith should not fail. So when you have repented and turned to me again, strengthen and build up your brothers.

Now my sister, take this scripture Luke 22:31-32 and make this personal. First write your name in these spaces below:
_____, Satan has asked to have all of you, to sift you like wheat. (32) But I have pleaded in prayer for you, _____, that your faith should not fail.

Second, the scripture directs us to turn to God. 'So when you have repented and turned to me again, strengthen and build up your brothers (Luke 22:32b)." You may ask yourself, "How does one turn to God?" To make God first in your life you have to seek and make room for God. Matthew 6:32b, 'Your heavenly Father already knows all your needs (33) and he will give you all you need from day to day if you live for him and make the Kingdom of God your primary concern.

Transform into your Jeremiah 29:11 identity by aligning your five senses to your Jeremiah 29:11 purpose. This season identify people with the Psalm 1:1 gifts and wisdom to help guide you in your Jeremiah 29:11 Path. These people are important to help you identify your strengths and weakness, become balanced, and study with you.

Still Point Moment: You have the ability to overcome any situation that hinders you. Remember in this path, Satan desires to shift you as wheat. Don't be afraid to be shaken and set apart from the crowd because God has already prayed for you to stay on this treasure guide to your Jeremiah 29:11 destiny.

Still Transition Affirmation: My strength is from the Lord. *May our Lord Jesus Christ and God our Father, who loved us and in his special favor gave us everlasting comfort and good hope (II Thessalonians 2: 16) (17) comfort your hearts and give you strength in every good thing you do and say.*

God's Plan for Women: Build Yourself, Home, and Children

Still Point: *O Lord, you have examined my heart and know everything about me. You know when I sit down or stand up. You know my every thought when far away. You chart the path ahead of me and tell me where to stop and rest. Every moment you know where I am (Psalm 139:1-3).*

The Lord is examining your heart. You can examine your heart and clear out negative mess hindering you from receiving messages and blessings from the Lord. This season, be encouraged and know that God has charted the Jeremiah 29:11 path ahead of you. The best is yet to come for you. Let me encourage you that you do not have to remain the way you are. There is a Jeremiah 29:11 seed within you that requires you to reach out and bless other people. Your reputation is important. Therefore, you want people to reach out and be a blessing towards others through the virtue and fruit that is within you. Therefore, it is important to have a clean heart. Let's examine the virtue of a woman. Don't praise yourself; let others do it (Proverbs 27:2)!

Proverbs 31:10, Who can find a virtuous and capable wife? She is worth more than precious rubies. (11) Her husband can trust her, and she will greatly enrich (favor) his life. (12) She will not hinder him but help him all her life. (13) She finds wool and flax and busily spins it. (14) She is like a merchant's ship; she brings her food from afar. (15) She gets up before dawn to prepare breakfast for her household and plan the day's work for her servant girls. (16) She goes out to inspect a field and buys it; with her earnings she plants a vineyard. (17) She is energetic and strong, a hard worker. (18) She watches for bargains; her lights burn late into the night. (19) Her hands are busy spinning thread, her fingers twisting fiber. (20) She extends a helping hand to the poor and opens her arms to the needy. (21) She has no fear of winter for her household because all of them have warm clothes. (22) She quilts her won bedspreads. She dresses like royalty in gowns of finest cloth. (23) Her husband is well known, for he sits in the council meeting with the other civic leaders. (24) She makes belted linen garments and sashes to sell to the merchants. (25) She is clothed with strength and dignity, and she laughs with no fear of the future. (26) When she speaks, her words are wise, and kindness is the rule when she gives instructions. (27) She carefully watches all that goes on in her household and does not have to bar the consequences of laziness. (28) Her children stand and bless her. Her husband praises her: (29) "There are many virtuous and capable women in the world, but you surpass them all!" (30) Charm is deceptive, and beauty does not last, but a woman who fears the Lord will be greatly praised. (31) Reward her for all she has done. Let her deeds publicly declare her praise.

This woman is compared to rubies. It takes searching, planning, and digging to find a ruby. Thus, it takes this same effort to find a wife and make a marriage work. The making of a wife and mother are part of your ministry. Also, this work and teaching must be modeled by virtuous women who love the Lord, their husbands, and children.

Rubies are beautiful jewels; however, it takes an explorer time to search and dig for these special stones. This exploration may take some time. A Godly husband is the finder. Therefore, a man seeking a wife will patiently wait and pray while establishing a home, savings, and income to provide. A wife is worth the wait once found by the husband. A husband can recognize his wife once he has security of a home and protection available. For example, once a ruby is found, it becomes a treasure for the finder. Similar finding and discovery are the same for a wife. *Proverbs 18:22, The man who finds a wife finds a treasure and receives favor from the Lord.* A wife must see her ministry to help and give birth to the vision of her husband's ministry. A wife helps her husband and children, and this ministry requires daily work. Woman of God, you are a treasure because you have a promise and purpose to be creative and give birth in ministry with your husband and family. This means that you have short and long-term goals to establish. In addition, you also have anniversaries and celebrations of the Jeremiah 29:11 missions and visions of your family and community members.

Be a wife that builds her house, works, takes care of children, and plans for the seasons ahead. Pray and build your house in the name of Jesus. Keep your husband, children, and household covered in the blood of Jesus. A woman that works is one who manages the house, rooms, and also one who builds. Most of all, she delegates authority with a schedule and routine. This skill requires awareness of the seasons, time management, and goal setting for the work that needs to be done. Be a wife and mother who takes care of her children by feeding, clothing, nurturing, and training them in the ways of the Lord. Therefore, it is important for the wife to know the difference between being wise versus foolish with her hands and mouth (Proverbs 14:1). A wife must take the following Proverbs into consideration to build her, family, and house:

1. **Do not nag!** (Proverbs 27:15) *A nagging wife is as annoying as the constant dripping on a rainy day. (16) Trying to stop her complaints is like trying to stop the wind or hold something with greased hands.*

2. **Be understanding.** (Proverbs 19:14) *Parents can provide their sons with an inheritance of houses and wealth, but only the Lord can give an understanding wife.*

3. **Be wise and build your house.** *A wise woman builds her house; a foolish woman tears hers down with her own hands* (Proverbs 14:1).

4. **Be your husband's joy and crown.** (Proverbs 12:4) *A worthy wife is her husband's joy and crown; a shameful wife saps his strength.*

5. **Be a fountain.** (Proverbs 5:18) *Let your wife be a fountain of blessing for you. Rejoice in the wife of your youth. (19) She is a loving doe, a graceful deer. Let her breast satisfy you always. May you always be captivated by her love. (20) Why be captivated, my son, with an immoral woman, or embrace the breasts of an adulterous woman?*

A wife is described as a treasure, crown, joy, and as a source of understanding. Get ready to change your mind, spirit, and environment to fulfill the Jeremiah 29:11 plans God has in mind.

Your ministry is to be a woman who builds herself, husband, and children. You can build your home to support the gifts and talents of your family as you minister and intercede; then, the Lord will reveal to you their Jeremiah 29:11 seeds to meet their conditions.

A wife is referred to as a good thing (Proverbs 18:22) and a fountain of blessing (Proverbs 5:18). This means that God created you to be skilled and exceptional with what you have. A fountain gives life and refreshes the habitat it surrounds. Therefore, you have the ability to give life and multiply the things that surround you. There are no limits to the things a woman can build or design in her home. A fountain of blessings can be referred to as the refreshment she brings to her home, family, and people after spending time with God. Spending time with God is key to remaining on the Jeremiah 29:11 path and understanding your purpose to build.

Understanding this purpose is important for managing your time with God and your family. Be a woman who understands herself, children, and husband by spending time with God. Allow God to guide and strengthen you to be a victorious and capable woman. Most of all, be a woman who speaks life into the Jeremiah 29:11 seeds in her children and family members.

Building your home in the place where you are will take hard work and dedication. Let me encourage you not to take shortcuts, but to develop good planning skills. *Good planning and hard work lead to prosperity, but hasty shortcuts lead to poverty (Proverbs 21:5).* Therefore, you have to make time to plan, save money, create new things, give things away, and move things around. God has given you the seed! All you need to do is value it and learn how to multiply the things you have. Learn to value gardening, cooking, sewing, and making goals.

Still Point Moment: Woman, it is important that you set the example and prepare and teach your children to be capable husbands and wives. It's imperative that our sons and daughters have household responsibilities to understand the value of home and family. Be encouraged as you continue in your Jeremiah 29:11 plans and as you build yourself, house, and family to support the gifts and talents from God.

Still Transition Affirmation: I will listen to the Spirit of God. So humble yourselves under the mighty power of God, and in His good time He will honor you (I Peter 5:6).

Section 1: Discovering Your Jeremiah 29:11 Plans and Path Reflection

Make room in your heart to listen to wisdom. God wants you to listen to wisdom in order to understand the plans He has for you. Wisdom will help you stay connected to your Jeremiah 29:11 assignment and provide guidance to exit or face obstacles.

If you tolerate a situation too long, it will not change. You will have to learn how to let go as you journey on your Jeremiah 29:11 plans. Some obstacles you may encounter or experience will cause you to leave people or places.

The seasons you will experience according to *Ecclesiastics Chapter 3* will be compared to a woman's pregnancy. Woman of God, there is a season coming when you have to let go and trust that every prayer invested for you and your children's future will come to pass.

We were first formed in God's womb, and planted in our mother's womb. From the womb, the baby develops an attachment and bond with the mother. The fetus learns to know his mother's voice and smell and develops emotions and reactions to his mother's environment. During the trimesters of pregnancy, there is a psychological, emotional, and behavioral attachment that develops between mother and fetus. After the season of pregnancy comes the labor. Contractions stretch the muscles to push the baby for the crowning position. From our mother's womb, we were crowned with a purpose. God has crowned your plan with a purpose.

In the delivery process, God stretches our purpose through each contraction. As we go through labor, He is equipping us with each push and every cry to go through our situation and finish to the end. Every scream, every tear, and every relationship is part of God's plan to prepare you for your delivery. *Ecclesiastes 3:2 states, "There is a time to be born and a time to die."* You will experience pain, life, and death (the end of a relationship) in the plans God has for you. Therefore, it is important that you give your pain, experience, and situation over to God.

As human beings, we have to grow both spiritually and naturally towards our purpose. Spiritually, we interact with the Holy Spirit through praise and worship, devotion, prayer and fasting, and walking by the fruit of the Spirit. Physically, we grow and develop into our being.

The plans God has for you are unfolded as you experience different relationships and interactions with others. Remember, there are spiritual people according to Ephesians 4:11 to help equip you to discover your purpose. Indeed, God wants us to have a relationship and discover our purpose.

1. What is your Jeremiah 29:11 purpose?
2. Did you recently discover your spiritual purpose?
3. What have you committed to during your Jeremiah 29:11 self-discoveries?
4. Do you recognize your gift or have considered other alternatives such as adoption, denial, or termination of your purpose?
5. Are you tired of the same cycles and patterns and repeated behaviors?

SECTION 2: DISCOVER GOD'S WISDOM

God's Plan for Women: Know your Season

Still Point: *There is a time for everything, a season for every activity under Heaven. A time to be born and a time to die. A time to plant and a time to harvest (Ecclesiastes 3:1-2).*

God is the Father of time and seasons. Our Heavenly Father created you with a purpose. Your gift is designed to be a generation builder for the Kingdom of God within your family and community. This should establish a ripple effect of heaven on earth connections from person to person, family to family, community to community, and generation to generation. The woman's role is important in the development of life and gifts with the children they are assigned to raise and teach. Women of God need to see all children as their responsibility to help develop, understand, and manifest their Jeremiah 29:11 identities. Also, women have a responsibility to give support to other mothers struggling to manage their households.

God has plans for children born out of wedlock. Therefore, it is important for women to have the perspective that God has plans for all children. You could be a woman responsible for a baby you did not carry or deliver; however, you've taken on the duty to care and raise the child. For example, after a child is born, feeding from the breast or bottle is the first lesson they are taught. The baby learns to open its mouth and use its mouth muscles to suck out the milk. After lesson number one, the baby develops a taste for the milk, but the mother has to determine when the baby is full. The mother has to burp the baby to prevent him/her from spitting up. Through these interactions, the child develops trust that his/her needs and demands will be met. Therefore, God has plans for women whether they are the natural mother or a caretaker to their assigned families within the church or the community.

There are going to be seasons as a family caretaker that you may experience challenges with the family or the child you are assigned to help. Therefore, it is important that women understand their roles as caregivers to children and their family members. Pray about your seasons to be in the lives of the children and families to whom you minister. Your seasons to help may be for special outings, birthdays, holidays, or back to school ministries. If not, your ministry could be to send encouraging cards or letters. It is important that you help the children or families within your community with no strings attached.

As mothers and caretakers, there are seasons to train up your children for Kingdom purposes. This becomes the time when mothers and caretakers have to plant the Word of God into their children. As mothers and caretakers, you have to plant and prepare the children for their harvest. In addition, you have to be responsible for training up children in the agape way. The agape way is loving children and families with a Godly approach. Love is key to having an agape way and approach. Wealth is in our children; therefore, they have to be trained up in the ways of the Lord. For in due season, your child will reap the prayers of harvest and have knowledge to sow into it.

1. **Be wise.** Prepare your home to become the training foundation to develop your children's gifts and talents with the following scriptures: *Fear of the Lord is the beginning of wisdom. Knowledge of the Holy One results in understanding* (Proverbs 9:10). *(11) Wisdom will multiply your days and add years to your life. (12) If you become wise, you will be the one to benefit. If you scorn wisdom, you will be the one to suffer.*

2. **Build your home.** A house is built by wisdom and becomes strong through good sense (Proverbs 24:3). *(4) Through knowledge its rooms are filled with all sorts of*

precious riches and valuables.   (5) A wise man is mightier than a strong man, and a man of knowledge is more powerful than a strong man.   (6) So don't go to war without wise guidance; victory depends on having many counselors.

3.   **Be a builder in the Kingdom**. *It is God's privilege to conceal things and king's privilege to discover them* (Proverbs 25:2). God's plan for women are to be caregivers and to build themselves, their homes, self, and their children. In this text, home means your body/temple. This starts with having wisdom and understanding of God's plan for you. You can gain wisdom about God by reading the Word about women who had the victory and prayed to God for answers. Patience is a required virtue in the plans God has for you. Praying and reading God's Word are foundations for understanding what God has for you and your children. Keep these things in mind while you continue to search and wait on your promise:

Questions:

1. What are the treasures have you discovered during your treasure hunt?
2. What is your purpose?
3. What new knowledge have you learned?
4. What does your crowd look at?

Still Point Moment: A time to harvest means that you need to test what you have sown in your children. Today you can make room in your heart and begin to listen for wisdom's instructions about how to raise your children, become a better mother, and build your home. Be the example you want your children to become. You can have new understanding with God's wisdom by reading and studying the Word. Let me encourage you to let go of your understanding and allow God to change you.

Still Transition Affirmation: I believe all things are possible. *Anything is possible if a person believes* (Mark 9:23b).

This is your season to know that all things are possible when you make room in your heart for faith to work. Believe and make room in your heart for God to mend and fix obstacles that challenge you and your family. You have the ability and what it takes to know and understand your Jeremiah 29:11 assignment. Build your relationship with God, yourself, and family at home through prayer, meditation, and the Bible.

God's Plan for Women: Use God's Wisdom

Still Point: *If you stop listening to instruction, my child, you have turned your back on knowledge* (Proverbs 19:27).

Listen to the Word of the Lord. Don't be like the woman named Folly. Who is Folly? Proverbs 9:13 describes a woman named Folly:

> *Folly is loud and brash. She is ignorant and doesn't' even know it. (14) She sits in her doorway on the heights overlooking the city. (15) She calls out to men going by who are minding their own business (16) "Come home with me," she urges the simple. To those without good judgment, she says, (17) "Stolen water is refreshing; food eaten in secret tastes the best!" (18) But the men don't realize that her former guests are now in the grave.*

Other scriptures pertaining to Folly include:

1. Proverbs 12:23 *Wise people don't make a show of their knowledge, but fools broadcast their folly.*

2. Proverbs 26:11 *As a dog returns to its vomit, so a fool repeats his folly.*

Women of folly do things in secret and set traps for the people that sit at their table. Watch out, because a woman of folly will reach into your plate without permission. God is watching! The information gathered about people of folly includes their lack self-control and discipline. Also, people of folly practice foolish behaviors that are mental traps. A life of folly, with no self-control and discipline, can hurt your relationships with people in your family or on the job. It is important for you to recognize the tables and traps set in your path. There is a table prepared for you to sit and listen to wisdom in the Jeremiah 29:11 plans God for you. Therefore, you have to spend time studying the Word of God and praying to understand and discern what is wise and what is folly.

The life of Ms. Folly can be a revolving door, lifestyle, and a trapped situation with heavy feet. It is a life without the quality of having knowledge and good judgment. God designed you with the quality of being wise and it is important for you to manage it. Let me encourage you to stay in the will of God and not be like Folly. Wisdom gives you discernment about what is right and wrong. It is your responsibility to make wise decisions to change and stay within the promises of God. The devil will set traps for you to get robbed, feel devalued, and defeated before God gives you the blessing. Therefore, it is important for you to evaluate the motives of people that want to be around you.

This is your season to cut the string of attachment to Folly; as well as people and thinkers like her and be a woman with wise answers. You will learn to speak in silence if you don't have an answer. Let me encourage you to be content with the things you have and not worry about the things not in your life. For example, you don't have to live a fake life that gives the impression that you have a lot of money when, in reality, you don't have money to pay monthly bills. Live within your means. If you don't have money for items you need, you can learn to save your money with a budget. It's time to get your finances in order with a plan. You need to have a strategic plan with goals in order to have success and be aware of traps.

As you continue to build yourself, children, and community, let God order your steps. Wisdom can keep your feet from walking and getting into situations of folly. The life of folly will breed obstacles that will spiral you down. You have the ability to embrace, re-think, and change the way you live and have relationship with others this season. You can let go of folly people when you "cut off" the strings of attachment and contact.

Changes in your lives can make the process of "let-go" and "cut-off" easier. Let me encourage you to embrace peace as you re-think changes this season. Start budgeting your income to prepare for the seasons ahead. Peace, joy, and understanding are the virtues you harvest once you receive wisdom. Wisdom is the reward you receive when you listen to God. You can know what to do next in your Jeremiah 29:11 plans with wisdom.

Still Point Moment: God has your answer. Sit at wisdom's table. Give your worries to God as you make room in your heart and mind. Embrace the plans God has for you to receive peace, joy, and other heavenly benefits in the Jeremiah 29:11 plans.

Still Transition Affirmation: I will seek the Lord. *The Lord God promises to deliver me from ALL my fears. If you look for me in earnest, you will find me when you seek me* (Jeremiah 29:13).

God's Plan for Women: Sit at Wisdom's Table

Still Point: *How can we understand the road we travel? It is the Lord who directs our steps* (Proverbs 20:24).

The Lord is directing your steps. In order to understand the plans God has for you, you have to ask for directions. You can make wrong decisions, get lost, or fall off track when you don't ask for directions. What makes a woman virtuous or like Folly? To answer this question is to discern the table where the woman is sitting. Also, it's important to know who set the table and their intentions for your company. Most of all, it is important to know what the inviter is serving.

(Proverbs 9:1) Wisdom has built her spacious house with seven pillars. (2) She has prepared a great banquet, mixed the wines, and set the table. (3) She has sent her servants to invite everyone to come. She calls out from the heights overlooking the city. (4) "Come home with me she urges the simple. To those without good judgment, she says, (5) "Come, eat my food, and drink the wine I have mixed. (6) Leave your foolish ways behind, and begin to live; learn how to be wise.

A virtuous woman is planted and connected to God. She abides in God's Word and Wisdom. A woman of folly does not have a plan of good intentions and her motives are self-centered. Her intentions are demanding and she wants to receive instant gratification for everything. It's important to recognize women of folly because their motives are to be takers instead of givers in every situation. Also, women of folly believe they are entitled to services, people, and places without a cost. Therefore, you need wisdom to discern women of folly. The primary motives of women like this are to gain attention and have their way in secret, cry, fib, and burst out in anger. Therefore, it is important that you resist Ms. Folly when she appears. You have to get tired of Ms. Folly in order to resist her. If you've encountered some of Ms. Folly's ways, you can confront them with the spirit of love. This means that you can pray for the person with a spirit of folly.

When are you going to get tired of Folly and sit down at wisdom's table? You don't have to make any reservations for this seating. Learning to be wise is learning how to listen, wait, and receive instruction from the Lord. Wisdom has set a table for those who search for these benefits: unending riches, honor, wealth, and justice belong to her to distribute (Proverbs 8:18). While you're sitting at wisdom's table, taste and see that the Lord is good. Let me encourage you to pull up a chair and sit at wisdom's table! The following scriptures describe the experience of sitting at wisdom's table.

1. *You prepare a feast for me in the presence of my enemies. You welcome me as a guest, anointing my head with oil. My cup overflows with blessings* (Psalm 23:5).

2. *Friendship with the Lord is reserved for those who fear him. With them he shares the secrets of his covenant* (Proverbs 25:14).

Where do you want your seat? With Folly or Wisdom? Do you want to be a builder or destroyer? You were never designed to be like Folly. You were made to be a winner which is why you can't remain the way you are!

1. **Step out.** You have to step out of it. Lose your appetite for lust and sin. Trust wisdom's ways for seeking God. Woman, trust wisdom's ways for finding your husband. *The humble will see their God at work and be glad. Let all who seek God's help live in joy* (Psalm 69:33).

2. **Wisdom is shelter.** Look for wisdom and make the Lord your shelter. Psalm 91:9, *If you make the Lord your refuge, if you make the Most High your shelter, (10) no evil will conquer you; no plague will come near your dwelling. (11) For he orders his angels to protect you wherever you go. (12) They will hold you with their hands to keep you from striking your foot on a stone.*

3. **Wisdom has instructions.** Listen for instructions. (Proverbs 2:2) *Tune your ears to wisdom, and concentrate on understanding.*

Let me encourage you to live in the joy of the Lord as you sit at wisdom's table. Wisdom is your shelter and gives instruction to keep you safe when you acknowledge the Lord in every situation. You need wisdom to have self-control. Proverbs clearly describes a wise person as one who follows wisdom and sits at her table. Pull up your chair to the table of wisdom to receive the ingredients you need to complete your Jeremiah 29:11 plans.

Sit at wisdom's table to receive the knowledge to keep your blessings and be a blessing to others. You need self-control to trust, look, and listen for instructions. You have to seek God to have this grace come upon you. Therefore, sit at wisdom's table to understand and prevail in the plans God has for you.

Still Point Moment: Turn away from folly and have a seat at wisdom's table. The plans God has for you are to prosper and have hope. Acting like Folly too long creates a "stuck" lifestyle with strongholds that grow from one thing into another. Free yourself from Ms. Folly and pull up a chair at Wisdom's table. *For the Lord sees clearly what a man does, examining every path he takes* (Proverbs 5:21*). (22) An evil man is held captive by his own sins; they are ropes that catch and hold him. (23) He will die for lack of self-control; he will be lost because of his incredible folly.*

Still Transition Affirmation: I am never alone because the Lord is my constant helper. *Knowledge of the Holy One results in understanding* (Proverbs 9:18).

God's Plans for Women: Recover

Still Point: *I love the Lord because he hears and answers my prayers* (Psalm 116:1). *(2) Because he bends down and listens, I will pray as long as I have breath!*

The Lord hears and answers prayers. Woman of God, life is packaged with weights of pain, discouragement, sorrow, loneliness, and fear. However, we have to count these obstacles all joy (James 1:1-3)! We have to be careful of the people we allow to sit at our tables. There are some people that we invite to sit at our tables who don't belong. Sometimes people will just sit down at your table only to take your bread and butter.

Eve, the first lady, can perhaps testify about the Lord. A major lesson learned from Eve is to be careful of the people at your table. Beware of the people and company you bring in your house. Most of all, be aware of snakes. How can you tell a snake? A snake is a deceiver, robber, and thief. Once you've encountered a snake, you start to notice things missing from your table, division in your house, and disagreements. A snakebite only brings poison in your house. Therefore, you have to be cautious of the table your enemy sets up for you.

(Genesis 3:17) And to Adam he said, "Because you listened to your wife and ate the fruit I told you not to eat, I have placed a curse on the ground. All your life you will struggle to scratch living from it. (18) It will grow thorns and thistles for you, though you will eat of its grains. (19) All your life you will sweat to produce food, until your dying day. (20) Then you will return to the ground from which you came. For you were made from dust, and to the dust you will return."

The adversary came to Eve in the form of a snake. As a result, she listened and lost dominion. However, God had a plan for our recovery. You have recovered from this snakebite! Jesus sacrificed himself so that you can recover from the bite! His blood covered you while He was on the cross! This season, you need to resist the snake! God will prepare you a table this season and you need to discern people and their intentions that suddenly appear in your garden.

Therefore, you need to find out their purposes before they sit down at your table.

Your flesh will return to the ground when you die, but your spirit will live. This spirit is alive in you to discern the motives and interests of others. Let me encourage you to evaluate the people around you. Boldly ask people if they know their Jeremiah 29:11 identities. A person like Folly only wants to take the blessings given and earnings you saved. Let me encourage you to pray and ask God for discernment to see the motives and intentions of others while you remain on your Jeremiah 29:11 path.

The Lord is always near and knows how you're feeling. Sometimes things happen suddenly without warning and impact your life in a negative way, but you can recover. You can recover from a snakebite or when people take advantage of you. God is in control of your recovery. Let God pick you up and mend the brokenness you experienced from a snakebite. God will make you whole again. All you have to do is forgive yourself and the other person. Most of all, it is important that you do not repeat the folly. You have what it takes to remain on your Jeremiah 29:11 path and purpose. The best is yet to come for you.

Still Point Moment: In the mist of everything, God is preparing you for your Jeremiah 29:11 plans and purpose. During this season, God wants to make you whole. You are designed to fulfill His word on earth.

Still Transition Affirmation: The LORD is my portion. *The Lord is my inheritance; therefore, I will hope in Him* (Lamentations 3:24).

God is seeking to fulfill His word on Earth. Call on God when you are feeling weak because the Lord is your portion and guide in your Jeremiah 29:11 assignments.

God's Plan for Women: Resist

Still Point: *Long ago, even before He made the world, God loved us and chose in Christ to be Holy and without fault in His eyes (Ephesians 1:4). (5) His unchanging plan has always been to adopt us into His own family by bringing us to Himself through Jesus Christ. And this gave Him blessings.*

Let's examine the book of Luke and celebrate our recovery and redemption from the trap of the snake. This same serpent that trapped the minds of Eve and Adam lost in the temptation of Jesus while He was fasting.

Luke 4:1, *The Jesus, full of the Holy Spirit, left the Jordan River. He was led by the Spirit to go out into the wilderness, (2) where the Devil tempted Him for forty days. He ate nothing all that time and was very hungry. (3) Then the Devil said to Him, "If you are the Son of God, change this stone into a loaf of bread." (4) But Jesus told him, "No! The Scriptures say, 'People need more than bread for their life.' (5) Then the Devil took him up and revealed to him all the kingdoms of the world in a moment of time. (6) The Devil took told Him, "I will give you the glory of these kingdoms and authority over them-because they are mine to give to anyone I please. (7) I will give it all to you if you bow down and worship me." (8) Jesus replied, "The Scripture say, 'You must worship the Lord your God; serve only Him.' (9) Then the Devil took Him to Jerusalem, to the highest point of the Temple, and said, "If you are the Son of God, jump off! (10) For the Scriptures say, 'He orders His angels to protect and guard you. (11) And they will hold you with their hands to keep you from striking your foot on a stone.'" (12) Jesus responded, "The Scriptures also say, 'Do not test the Lord you God.'" (13) When the Devil had finished tempting Jesus, he left him until the next opportunity came.*

Jesus went into the wilderness to be tempted for forty days. The adversary appeared three times to test Jesus. Jesus overpowered the adversary with the Word of God. During this test, Jesus had you on His mind. God has written in your Jeremiah 29:11 identity that you will be resilient. Victory is written in your Jeremiah 29:11 plans over any temptation. The Lord has already prayed for your strength to stand, win, and overcome any situation or weapon formed! Be encouraged and know that God gave you the victory to overcome any temptation.

There is a fountain of living water in you that is connected to your Jeremiah 29:11 seed. Jesus is the living water and fountain connection that will replenish you and help you overcome temptation. This season, be a fountain of praise and wisdom to others. Also, realize you are a revelation! In the Garden of Eden, the woman was known as Adam's revelation, "bone of my bone, flesh of my flesh." However, sin caused them to separate their oneness, because the woman was given a name and purpose. You have the authority in Jesus to resist any temptation. There are consequences for not yielding and evaluating your situation. Giving into the temptation can affect your health and home as well as the people you are called to minister to and save.

The adversary does not want you to discover your Jeremiah 29:11 seed and responsibilities. There are responsibilities that stem from being a woman. First, it is important to understand that being a caretaker, wife, or mother is a ministry. A wife has to keep her household and husband covered in prayer at all times. The main responsibility is to pray for your household—especially your family members. Our wombs and mouths are designed to give life to our seeds and not to destroy or tear down people's spirits. Woman of God, you must understand your purpose as a caretaker, wife, or mother. It is written that a woman is a suitable companion for a man (Genesis 2:20). Also, a wife is to submit to her husband (Ephesians 5:22). Therefore, a mother is to sow the Word of God and teachings into her children. As a result, in due season, as the child grows they will reap a harvest and be equipped for spiritual warfare. Be a woman that spends time with God and who is not afraid to resist temptation.

The adversary has a plan to keep you from discovering your Jeremiah 29:11 seed. Therefore, it is important for you to resist any temptation and apply the Word of God in your life daily. The Word of God is a sword of truth against the adversary. You can recover what you think you lost when you re-try and re-build. Don't be afraid to re-try and re-build this season.

Still Point Moment: Embrace a new lifestyle. Make room to hear when God is talking to you as you continue to walk in the plans God has for you. God has a table set up for you to eat, drink, and get refreshed to build up the Kingdom. Wisdom is near you, speaking to your heart when you are still. Stay encouraged as you recover and walk in the plans God has for you.

Still Transition Affirmation: I will have hope. *Lord, sustain me as you promised that I might live!* (Psalm 119:116). The Lord is your portion and answer in your Jeremiah 29:11 assignments. God will be your portion as you make room in your heart and have hope in the plans for you.

God's Plan for Women: Be a Light

Still Point: *The steps of the godly are directed by the Lord. He delights in every detail of our lives* (Psalm 37:23). *Though they stumble, they will not fall, for the Lord holds them by hand (24).*

God is directing your steps and holding your hand right now. Get ready! Get your mind and heart ready because you will not fall. Let me encourage you to remember that God knows what's best for you in the plans and purpose for your life. Let God direct your steps this season. Also, speak, "Let there be light" in every situation.

According to the Apostle John, our Heavenly Father created everything with the command, "Let there be light." This light has a purpose on Earth and in Heaven. The book of Genesis describes how God created Heaven, Earth, man and woman, and good and evil. God declared, "Let there be" and "Let us make" and the Creator designed our Jeremiah 29:11 in the beginning. Adam and Eve lived in the Garden of Eden for some time before eating from the Tree of Knowledge. During this time, Adam and Eve dwelled, worshiped, worked, and walked with God. I can imagine that Eden was a paradise filled with an overflow of abundance with fruit trees and green valleys.

I can imagine God, Adam, and Eve spending time talking and walking through the high and low of the mountains. I believe there were tall trees that shaded the grass and gardens of vegetables and flowers that covered the grounds. In Eden, I can imagine treasure, gold, and silver above ground. I can see Adam and Eve as one before *"the eyes of both of them were opened* (Genesis 3:7a)."

Let me encourage you to declare, "Let there be light," to the plans God has for you. You need light to have a revelation and understanding of what you see and who is talking to you. Let's look at Adam and Eve's temptation. Did Eve have revelation of the serpent? Did Eve have understanding about the Tree of Knowledge of Good and Evil? It's important that we stay on guard by examining what others are trying to shake, share, take, or exchange with us.

What I mean by staying on guard is to keep God, His truth, His Word first, and to always use discernment. Ask God to show you a person's intentions. The scriptures say that we shall know people by their fruits. Test a spirit by the spirit by speaking, "Let there be light," so that you are not tricked, fooled, betrayed, and deceived by the things others are saying.

Adam and Even lost their treasure because they believed what they perceived from the serpent. They agreed with the serpent instead of agreeing with God. The serpent's plan was to kill, steal, and destroy Adam's destiny and take his possessions and access. Adam's dominion was in the Garden of Eden. Adam lost his dominion when he disobeyed God and ate of the fruit (Genesis 3:7a). Can you imagine how Adam and Eve were feeling at this time? I believe they realized they were tricked the moment their eyes were opened. Also, I believe Adam felt this loss of position as the Garden of Eden's manager. For the first time, Adam felt a sense of void, loss, and nakedness that was everything God's protection covered.

Also, Adam and Eve immediately looked at each other differently after eating the fruit and receiving revelation. They realized that they did something wrong. Their revelation was that they disobeyed and robbed God, *"They realized they were naked, they sewed fig leaves together and made coverings for themselves"* (Gen 3:7b). Even though Adam and Eve were evicted from the Garden, they did not lose their light. Life for Adam and Eve was harder, but they recovered.

Let's examine Adam and Eve's reaction to Genesis 3:7. First we must recognize that Adam and Eve were convinced to sin, made a decision to taste the fruit, and covered up together. They even tried to hide from God (Genesis 3:10). You can't hide from God. He is an all-knowing God. Women of God, what are you covering up? What are you trying to hide from God and from others? God sees everything.

Adam and Eve fell from their Eden duties but God's original plan continued. The principles of work, dominion, ethics, tithes, and offering continued in Adam and Eve's new life. This implies that they knew God's plan. They were witnesses, and they didn't lose their memories after they were evicted out of the garden. There are going to be many experiences that will test us, just like Adam and Eve; however, *"God in his mercy has given us this wonderful ministry; we never give up"* (II Corinthians 4:1)." Conceive a never give up spirit! Let me encourage you to allow God's glory to shine in the Jeremiah 29:11 plans for you. Let God's glory be revealed for others to be blessed and have hope in their future.

Eve was faced with obstacles; however, she remained connected to God. Jesus shows us how to resist the devil when we are tempted. Most of all, we cannot just live on bread alone. The fall of Adam/man was a result of rebellion and a broken covenant; however, God has been consistent with everlasting grace, mercy, and repentance.

I am focusing on Eve due to her role as the first created woman—a living resident in the Garden of Eden, a wife, a mother, and a grandmother. After being banished from Eden, Adam and Eve started a family, Genesis 4:1 *"Eve gave birth to Cain, and she said, "With the Lord's help, I have brought forth a man.* (Genesis 4:2) *Later she gave birth to a second son and named him Abel."* Her character as a mother is evident in the fact that she taught and nurtured her son's Cain, Abel, and Seth.

God continued to provide for Adam and Eve after their loss of dominion. Adam and Eve labored and produced offerings for God. They used the skills they learned in the Garden of Eden in their outside land to produce what they knew from Eden. They brought their worship and offerings into the fields and, as they began to build a harvest, Adam and Eve still put God first. As the first family, they were witnesses and continued to walk in the principles of worship after God banished them from the garden (Genesis 3:23). And their sons Cain and Abel brought offerings to God (Genesis 4:3). This implies that Adam and Eve taught them about God and of the necessity of developing a worship relationship with God. In addition to the purpose of labor, Abel became a shepherd while Cain was a farmer (Genesis 4:2). Adam and Eve engaged with their sons and taught them the values of labor and offering.

Eve had struggles and her sons inherited some of those attitudes and behaviors. Sadly, she witnessed Cain's sentenced to banishment for murdering Abel. She experienced losing two sons at the same time. After the death of Abel and Cain's banishment, Eve became pregnant and gave birth to another son. She named him Seth for she said, "God has granted me another son in place of Abel, the one Cain killed." The Lord restored Eve, and she had a revelation to rebuild her family. She had another chance to be restored as a mother.

I can imagine Eve telling Seth about his older brothers. As a mother, how do you believe Eve mourned in her moments thinking about her sons? Could you imagine losing two sons in the same day?

She lost one son by banishment and the other to murder. The death of Abel was the first death, murder, and bloodshed in human history. Cain's banishment is the second generation of eviction and banishment.

As Eve examined her situation, she felt empty; however, she knew God never abandoned her. I believe that she prayed for "light" and strength in her grief. Then she felt strength in her struggle and believed in a merciful God. I believe she raised and covered Seth differently. Eve taught and trained Seth differently than she did Cain and Abel. I can imagine Eve telling Seth about God, the Garden of Eden, the devil, and the differences between good and evil. When Seth grew up, he had a son and named him Enosh. It was during his lifetime that people first began to worship the Lord (Genesis 4:26). Seth's seed began a generation that followed and began to seek God and His ways; and they were trained in the directions they went (Proverbs 22:6). It is written that nine generations after Seth followed God. Noah was birthed from this bloodline. Seth's bloodline was protected in the ark during the flood. Then, eleven generations after Noah, Abraham made a covenant with God.

Woman of God, let me encourage you to pray and recognize God's purpose in our children and to train them in the ways of the Lord. Today, declare "light" on your Jeremiah 29:11 path and begin a new work with your purpose. Let me encourage to you declare, "Let there be light" in every situation and conversation. Exchange the Word of God through the kinds of fruits that are in us: love, joy, peace, patience, kindness, goodness, faithfulness, gentleness, and self-control (Galatians 5:22). Keep God first in every situation and use discernment by examining the fruit others bring.

Declaring, "Let there be light," will reveal truth. The truth will reveal where you are in God's will and the plans God has for you. Like Eve, you do not need to remain where you are! Eve's experience makes it clear that God is faithful and will restore you! You can recover from being tricked, deceived, and lied on. Declare, "Let there be light" and have hope in your future that God will reveal and release His glory upon you. Let me encourage you to stay strong when obstacles arise. Eve was a strong woman because she did not give up as a wife or a mother. Today, God is calling you to become engaged to His word with faith and submission in order to discover your purpose. Answer to the light God made and placed in you to keep the faith. This journey to discover your treasures and gifts waits for you as you begin to seek God. Understand that trauma and crisis can affect how you perceive life and regain hope. Biblically speaking about Eve, I believe her expectations of child rearing were no different from other Biblical women. Eve had a "never give up" spirit.

Adam was a priest and prophet; therefore, he had the gift to name. *Then Adam named his wife Eve, because she would be the mother of all people everywhere (Genesis 3:20). (21) And the Lord God made clothing from animal skins for Adam and his wife* and revealed her ministries of being a woman (Genesis 3:13, 16), wife (Genesis 2:25, 3:17), mother, and caretaker to rebuild her family and generations. I believe these revelations gave Eve hope and faith in God when she experienced challenges. Most of all, God continued to provide and made their clothing. God loves us more than we deserve. Let me encourage you that God is your portion and provider in your Jeremiah 29:11 assignment. Therefore, never give up because God has plans for you!

Being a Woman has many ministry positions such as a mother (Eve, Sarai/Sarah, and Mary mother of Jesus), wife (Rebekah), daughter, grandmother, aunt, neighbor (Jael), cousin (Elizabeth), Rebekah's favor towards Jacob (Genesis 25:28), and social member of community (Deborah and the many women that followed Jesus) who built and strengthened their children for Kingdom purposes. You can recover from a snakebite or trauma with a never give-up spirit. Therefore, walk in victory knowing that God is not finished with you yet!

Still Point Moment: Let me encourage you that there are many lessons we can learn from Eve such as never give up, pray, and rejoice. The consequences of not keeping God first can result in a loss of position, place, and possession. This is why it is important to be conscious of God's word and ways. I've been in situations where I felt fearful, ashamed, and lonely after being deceived, tricked, and fooled. In these situations, I prayed for God's rescue. From my own experiences, my eyes were opened after receiving knowledge from sermons, teachings, and Biblical studying materials to get myself out of the pit and back into position for the Jeremiah 29:11 plans. The truth and conviction can align us to the Word of God and the righteous path. When we act out on faith and believe in the will of

God, there is an immediate uncovering of Grace. God is faithful and will fulfill all He promises.

Still Transition Affirmation: I have everything I need. And God will generously provide you all you need. Then you will always have everything you need and plenty left over to share with others (2 Corinthians 9:8).

God is everything that you need as you continue to have faith. Declare light in your situation and believe that God will supply all your needs as you continue to become more determined in you Jeremiah 29:11 assignments.

Section 2: Discover God's Wisdom Still Point Reflection

God is in control of your seasons in the Jeremiah 29:11 plans for you. Activate your Jeremiah 29:11 seed and plans by connecting with God through prayer. You have the self-control to resist a seat or food from Folly's table and sit at Wisdom's table. God is going to test your obedience when faced with obstacles. However, we must trust God in those things we struggle to overcome. Let me encourage you to claim the victory and not the struggle.

God is with you in every season. Therefore, you are not alone. You may have a crowd around you, but you have to seek the Lord. The crowd around you will either crown or crowd the Jeremiah 29:11 plans God has for you. Evaluate your crowd, find those individuals who pray, support, and add to your purpose. God has so much for you! The key point is that Jesus is already in your path and your situation is already worked out to give you victory.

God made you in His image with gifts and talents to face any obstacle. You are never alone when you sit at His table. God is your answer to understanding the Jeremiah 29:11 plans. Continue to walk in victory with a never give-up spirit.

You belong to God
Identify the crowd members around you
God will bless you in front of the crowd
Trust in what God says
Sit at Wisdom's table
You can recover

SECTION 3: CHOSEN FOR MINISTRY

God's Plan for Women: Stay in My Will

Still Point: *For he issued his decree to Jacob; he gave his law to Israel. He commanded our ancestors to teach them to their children, (Psalm 78:5) so the next generation might know them-even the children not yet born-that they in turn might teach their children (6).*

The gifts of women who worship and teach their children prepare them for generational Jeremiah 29:11 assignments. The cycle of teaching and training is an act that passes on history, traditions, and cultures from parents to children. This helps each generation learn about God, obedience, and hope for the future. Jesus taught men and women the secrets of the Kingdom and how to have authority on Earth. Therefore, both genders have Jeremiah 29:11 ministry assignments in their homes, with their families, and throughout their communities.

Matthew 10:1 *Jesus called his twelve disciples to him and gave them authority to cast out evil spirits and to heal every kind of disease and illness.*

Jesus healed and delivered women within the crowds where He walked. After deliverance, some of these women stayed and followed the ministry. Matthew 26:6-13 describe a phenomenal woman and how she worshipped and gave honor to Jesus. She had a revelation of who Jesus was. Let's examine this woman together.

Meanwhile, Jesus was in Bethany at the home of Simon, a man who had leprosy (Matthew26:6). (7) During supper, a woman came in with a beautiful jar of expensive perfume and poured it over his head. (8) The disciples were indignant when they saw this, "What a waste of money," they said. (9) "She could have sold it for a fortune and given the money to the poor." (10) But Jesus replied, "Why berate her for doing such a good thing to me? (11) You will always have the poor among you, but I will not be here with you much longer. (12) She has pured this perfume on me to prepare my body for burial. (13) I assure you, wherever the Good News is preached throughout the world, this woman's deed will be talked about in her memory.

1. Why did Jesus and his disciples have supper in Simon's house?
2. What deed did Jesus say she will be remembered by?
3. What was her name?

This woman is phenomenal. Notice that a name is not written; however, her deed will be remembered. You must understand that your gift is always on assignment. Jesus had many assignments to fulfill during His time on Earth so that the people would believe in Him and turn to God. One lesson that you can learn from Jesus is that food becomes secondary when it is time to worship. Jesus knew this woman was coming because He is Jesus. The lesson that He wanted the disciples to notice was how this woman fulfilled her duty. There are going to be times in your Jeremiah 29:11 journey that your plans will get interrupted. However, you have to realize that your gifts and talents are always on duty.

This woman had a Jeremiah 29:11 assignment to appear in Simon's house with new oil to anoint Jesus. Then, she broke open a new bottle of oil and poured it on Jesus' head. She never spoke a word. I believe this woman had many purposes to worship Jesus. Maybe, she had witnessed one of Jesus' sermons, miracles, or deliverences. It's possible this woman's ministry was to visit the sick and shut-in. This woman may have worked for Simon as a nurse or maid-servant. Or, perhaps she was relative or a resident/guest of the house. These 'what ifs'do not matter! Her desire to worship Jesus while everyone else was eating was phenomenal.

This woman's worship is her revelation of Jesus. Worship is a reflection of revelation about your relationship with Jesus. Jesus can be revealed in a new way when things are bad or broken in your life. Therefore, don't be afraid when challenges or obstacles take place in your life. Jesus can begin something new in your life when you or something is broken. Are you willing to give up something you love or things considered valuable/expensive? When you are spritually broken and give Jesus your best, you can expect it to be returned to you or your family in a new way. All you need to do is trust Jesus as a healer, deliever, and minister. This woman knew Jesus was the Son of God. Her worship is an awarenes of their relationship. Jesus interpreted for His disciples because they did not understand her act of worhsip, love, and revelation. The desciples were indignant and made comments because of their misbeliefs and disortions. They did not have the same revelation of Jesus even though they had seen the miracles, heard His sermons, and received training.

This woman's actions were courageous because she was the only one with a revelation. This woman gave her best worship and offering in exchange for nothing. There are going to be people in the same place as you, who do not have the same principles you stand for, and do not understand the way you worship; however, Jesus does! Some people were at the place where Jesus was; however, they did not show up to give their service. They made a choice to hold on to their beautiful things. Yet, this phonomeanal woman came in during supper, at Simon's house, with her beautiful jar of expensive perfume and poured it over His head (Matthew 26:7). You can discover your Jeremiah 29:11 assignment and have a relationship and worship with Jesus. Let me encourage you to express your love, gifts, and telents freely in your Jeremiah 29:11 plans and purpose. Most of all, give God the glory.

Still Point Moment: This woman is phenomenal because her timing and assignment were to prepare Jesus' body for the burial with new oil from the bottle. I want to encourage you to be like this woman. Jesus is with your Jeremiah 29:11 plans and path. Others in the room may not understand what you're doing, but Jesus knows. The illustration of this worship is that you are just like the beautiful jar. You are creatively and wonderfully made for a purpose. God has blessed you with oil to operate in your purpose. Trust God, He will add oil to your flame when you seek and worship Him.

Still Transition Affirmation: I have everything I need in God. *Our only power and success come from God (2 Corinthians 3:5).*

Make room in your heart and mind to be a worshipper and operate in your purpose. God designed you with gifts and talents to operate in your purpose. God has given you everything you need to face obstacles and challenges.

God's Plan for Women: Have Faith

Still Point: *O my people, listen to my teaching. Open your ears to what I am saying,* (Psalm 78:1) *(2) for I will speak to you in a parable. I will teach you hidden lessons from our past (3) stories we have heard and know, stories our ancestors handed down from to us. (4) We will not hide these truths from our children but will tell the next generation about the glorious deeds of the Lord.*

It is important that you share the truths about the glorious deeds of the Lord. Let's examine Mary, Martha, and Lazarus' encounter with Jesus. We can learn a lot from their experiences.

Luke 10:(38) *As Jesus and the disciples continued on their way to Jerusalem, they came to a village where a women named Martha welcomed them into her home. (39) Her sister, Mary, sat at the Lord's feet listening to what he taught. (40) But Martha was worrying over the big dinner she was preparing. She came to Jesus and said, "Lord, doesn't it seem unfair to you that my sister just sits here where I do all the work? Tell her to come and help me." (41) But the Lord said to her, "My dear Martha, you are so upset over all these details! (42) There is really only one thing worth being concerned about. Mary had discovered it-and I won't take it away from her.*

Jesus came to visit his friends Mary, Martha, and Lazarus. During this visit, Martha worried about preparing the dinner instead of sitting where Jesus was teaching. Martha got upset about what she thought Mary should be doing to help. Mary sat at the Lord's feet listening to what He taught. Jesus revealed that Mary had discoved what needed to be taught to have faith. I can imagine Mary taking in the lessons and revelations about the Kingdom of God. Martha had other plans for Mary. Yet did she relized that she missed Mary's discovery worrying over dinner. It appears that Mary gave Jesus her undivided attention to receive what was next. The scriptures do not state how long Jesus taught, but I can imagine that Mary received a revelation and became a follower. Make time this season to hear from Jesus. Like Mary, you can sit at the feet of Jesus and discover God's plans. Understanding the Kingdom of God is priority over preparing and worrying about food. The teaching that Mary received helped her to call on Jesus when her brother Lazarus died. When she witnessed the resurrection of Lazarus, her worship ascended to another level.

God opened the witnesses' eyes to believe in Jesus through Lazarus' resurrection. After Jesus told them to roll the stone away, He shouted, *"Lazarus to come out (John 11:43)." And Lazarus came out, bound in grave clothes, his face wrapped in a head cloth. Jesus told them, "Unwrap him and let him go (44)!"*

Jesus is calling you to Him. You thought your situation was over, but Jesus has something for you. God wants you to have hope and prosper in your future. Roll the stone away from areas of your mind so that God can use you. Like Lazarus, Mary, and Martha, we have to make room for Jesus in our lives and homes. God wants to use you like he used them so others can believe in Jesus. Your worship is because of your relationship with Jesus. Give the Lord advanced praise for the future miracles and broken cycles in your family according to the Jeremiah 29:11 path you are living in today.

Mary's Revelation

John 12:1 *Six days before the Passover ceremonies began, Jesus arrived in Bethany, the home of Lazarus-the man he had raised from the dead. (2) A dinner was prepared in Jesus' honor. Martha served, and Lazarus sat at the table with him. (3) Then Mary took a twelve-once jar of expensive perfume made from essence of nard, and she anointed Jesus' feet with it and wiped his feet with her hair. And the house was filled with fragrance. (4) But Judas Iscariot, one of his disciples-the one who would betray him-said, (5) "That perfume was worth a small fortune. It should have been sold and the money given to the poor." (6) Not that he cared for the poor-he was a thief who was in charge of the disciples' funds, and he often took some for his own use. (7) Jesus replied, "Leave her alone. She did it in preparation for my burial. (8) You will always have the poor among you, but I will not be here with you much longer."*

Jesus was in the house of Mary and Martha after raising Lazarus from the dead. This second dinner occasion was in honor of Jesus. As Martha served, Lazarus sat the table, but Mary began to gather her perfume to pour on Jesus' feet. Mary had worship in mind because she was up close for Lazarus' miracle. Even though Jesus understood her worship, other people in the house that witnessed

Lazarus' funeral and resurrection did not join in to worship with Mary. Mary was once again at Jesus' feet; however, this time she anointed Jesus' feet with oil and wiped his feet with her hair. This experience took Mary's praise to the next level. As you believe in and serve Jesus, your praise and worship will go to another level.

The scarifical of oil showed that she wanted to anoint Jesus with something that was of great worth. In this situation, food was secondary for Mary. Mary expressed her revelation of Jesus through her worship and by giving up her best praise. God wants you to always give Him the glory! While you are on your Jeremiah 29:11 path, you need to always give God the glory in every situation. This means that you have to believe and conceive the plans God has for you. You have to take on the image of God. There is a Jeremiah 29:11 seed in you to do something for somebody else.

Let me encourage you to give God your best no matter who's in the room. Mary is phenomenal because of her revelation and timing. Give God your best while on your treasure quest towards your Jeremiah 29:11 purpose. A lesson to learn from Mary's would be to position yourself at Jesus' feet. We should take Mary's innocent position to sit at Jesus feet daily for meditation and prayer time. Mary is a phenomenal woman because of her faith in Jesus. Martha believed Jesus was the resurrection and the Messiah, the Son of God, and the one who had come into the world from God. Let me encourage you to be childlike, have a servant heart, and humble like Mary and Martha to discover the plans God has for you.

Still Point Moment: Jesus is calling you out of the situation that wants to consume you. Make room in your house to serve like Martha. Set a place for Jesus in your lives and homes. Lazarus sat at the table with Jesus. Do you realize that Jesus has prepared a table and chair for you? Victory is yours to have in the Jeremiah 29:11 purpose for your life.

Still Transition Affirmation: I have hope in the God. *So be strong and take courage, all you who put your hope in the Lord.* (Psalm 31:24).

Give Jesus your best. Be teachable as you continue in the plans God has for you. Make room in your heart to sit at Jesus' feet to pray, listen, or worship so you'll understand and have hope in your Jeremiah 29:11 assignments.

God's Plan for Women: Be Messengers

Still Point: *Sing a new song to the Lord, he has done wonderful deeds. He has won a might victory by his power and holiness* (Psalm 98:1). *(2) The Lord has announced his victory and has revealed his righteousness to every nation! (3) He has remembered his promise to love and be faithful to Israel. The whole earth has seen the salvation of our God.*

You will have a new song to sing when you follow Jesus. I can imagine the new songs and messages the woman shared with others. What is your new song? Let me encourage you to begin to celebrate and rejoice with others when the Lord's blessings are making instant changes and miracles in others.

Luke 8 *(1) Not long afterward Jesus began a tour of the nearby cities and villages to announce the Good New concerning the Kingdom of God. He took his twelve disciples with him, (2) along with some women he had healed and from whom he had cast out evil spirits. Among them were Mary Magdalene, from whom he had cast out seven demons; Joanna, the wife of Chuza, Herod's business manager; Susanna; and many others who were contributing from their own resources to support Jesus and his disciples.*

There were women who followed Jesus. Why did women follow Jesus? What revelations did they know about Jesus? What did they receive from being in the presence of the Lord? Jesus healed their brokeness. Once Jesus healed them, their ministries and Jeremiah 29:11 identities were revealed. These women's lives were transformed after their encounter with Jesus. I believe their obstacles and lifestyles changed when they followed Jesus as He went into the synagogues and taught the people. Many people were amazed by his teachings, casting out of evil spirits, and healing of the sick. Once people heard about the teachings and miracles, they came to Jesus to be healed and made whole. However, some people in the crowd were spectating and critically doubting Jesus.

Jesus was the teacher, leader, and deliverer of these women. I can only imagine the emptiness these women felt as they witnessed the cruxifiction and death of Jesus who once delivered and saved them. Their deliverance led many people to believe and recognize

Jesus. I believe these women messengers brought a message to unbelivers. They were a team of evangelists who spread the Word of God and reached out to love, help, and support for the Kingdom agenda.

These women were reformed through personal relaionship with Jesus. Thy were committed and understood their Jeremiah 29:11 plans. After Jesus' death, the women followed and watched and cared for him while he was in Galilee. Also, other women had come with him to Jerusalem such as, *Mary Magdalene, Mary (the mother of James the younger and of Joseph), and Salome* (Mark 15:40). *Zebedee's wife, the mother of James and John* (Matthew 27:56; (Luke 23:48-49).

Luke 23:(55) *As his body was taken away, the women from Galilee followed and saw the tomb where they placed his body. (56) Then they went home and prepared spices and ointments to embalm him. But by the time they were finished it was the Sabbath, so they rested all that day as required by the law.*

These women had Jeremiah 29:11 assignments and messages. They remained with Jesus after the crowd left and as the body of Jesus was transfered to the tomb. Then, the women made the spices to embalm Jesus' body and rested because of the Sabbath. Like these women, you have a Jeremiah 29:11 purpose which is to be followers of Christ and to carry out Jeremiah 29:11 assignments. These women's actions are an example of unity. They were willing to get the job done and got up early the next morning to serve.

These phenomenal women were followers of Jesus' minstry. They did not abandon their committment to their assignment after His death. These women were courageous during a moment of grief. I can imagine these women saw these events and witnessed to others with similar obstacles from which they were delivered. After the resurection, Jesus spoke to these women and gave them an amazing report to tell the other disciples and followers. Understand that when you follow Jesus' commands and directions, you are activating faith for your Kingdom assignment. Because of what they had seen, Jesus made them evangelists and witnesses of His ministry, death, and resurrection. These women are phenomenal because of their obedience to give service. You, too, have a message that you can share with others about Jesus.

Still Point Moment: These women became commited to their Jeremiah 29:11 assignment. You can become committed to the plans God has for you by planting God's message in your path and that of others. These women prayed together and spread the seed of God's message. Therefore, you have to know your gifts to either teach, preach, pray, or help others in their times of needs.

Still Transition Affirmation: God is our deliverer. *Come, let us tell of the Lord's greatness; let us exalt His name together* (Psalm 34:3).

God wants you to have hope and faith while you walk in your Jeremiah 29:11 assignment. You can have hope and overcome any situation, obstacle, or challenge. Most of all, you can encourage and help somebody in their time of need. You were designed to be a blessing to others as they complete their Jeremiah 29:11 assignment.

God's Plan for Women: Serve and Witness

Still Point: *Come, let us worship and bow down. Let us kneel before the Lord our maker,* (Psalm 95:6) *(7) for he is our God. We are the people He watches over, the sheep under His care. Oh, that you would listen to His voice today.*

God wants you to connect with others and share your new songs and messages. Let's examine the Samaritian woman's interaction with Jesus at the well as she listened to the voice of Jesus. Be encouraged as you realize that Jesus will show up in your path.

Soon a Samaritan woman came to draw water, and Jesus said to her, "Please give me a drink." John 4(8) He was alone at the time because his disciples had gone into the village to buy some food. (9) The woman was surprised, for Jews refused to have anything to with Samaritans. She said to Jesus, "You are a Jew, and I am a Samaritan woman. Why are you asking me for a drink?" (10) Jesus replied, "If you only knew the gift God has for you and who I am, you would ask me, and I would give you living water." (11) "But sir, you don't have a rope or a bucket," she said, "and this is a very deep well. Where would you get this living water?" (12) And besides, are you greater than our ancestor Jacob who gave us this well? How can you offer better water than he and his sons and his cattle enjoyed?"

A nameless Samaritan woman came to the well to fill her water jug. She noticed Jesus, but didn't know Him. This woman was shocked that Jesus asked her to serve Him. Jesus said to this woman, *"Please give me a drink"* (John 4:8). Jesus is asking the woman to serve Him. The exchange for serving/worshiping Jesus is a reward. Jesus also replied, *"If you only knew the gift God has for you and who I am, you would ask me, and I would give you living water"* (John 4:10). The gifts God has for you is priceless. All you have to do is make room for Him in your heart, mind, and body daily.

First, Jesus asked her to serve Him. She recognized that He was a Jew; however, the custom was that Jews did not interact with Samaritans. So Jesus broke the custom division by asking this woman to serve, ask, and trust Him. Jesus is asking you to serve, ask, and trust Him as you continue to walk on your Jeremiah 29:11 path.

---

(13) Jesus replied, "People soon become thirsty again after drinking this water. (14) But the water I give them takes away thirst altogether. It becomes a perpetual spring within them, giving them eternal life. (15) "Please sir," the woman said, "give me some of that water! Then I'll never be thirsty again, and I won't have to come here to haul water." (16) "Go and get your husband," Jesus told her. (17) "I don't have a husband, "the woman replied. Jesus said, "Your right! You don't have a husband (18) for you have five husbands, and you aren't even married to the man you're living with now."

Second, this woman thought the living water being referred to was the regular water the in the well. Then, she made the connection who Jesus was and began to thirst after Him. Jesus is telling this woman to believe, drink from His fountain well, put the water jugs down (your burdens), and become a follower.

Third, this woman had a revelation. She knew a little to connect with the relevant and, thus, had a revelation. Recognize the exchange between Jesus and this woman. This exchange was her routine of dry wells for Jesus' living fountain which required her to serve, worship, and believe in Him.

I can image that going to this well was a normal routine for this woman. In addition, the results were the hopes to find something to drink. I believe this woman was tired of her personal patterns and situations. The water jug she was carrying represents the weight of her tiredness but her walk showed her determination to leave her situation. Her conversation indicates that she recognizes that she is having a conversation with a Jew but does not realize she is talking to Jesus. Jesus asked this woman for a drink and as He offers His drink, she questions His ability to supply her with living water. This woman experienced instant change when Jesus reveled that He was the Messiah. Most of all, she brought people to meet Jesus.

When this woman came to the well, she was carrying her water jar. I believe living with different men was her pattern and lifestyle. In verse 28, after receiving the revelation that she was speaking to the prophet, she forgot about her purpose of going to the well. Why do you think she left the water jug? After talking with Jesus, she found her purpose to witness and share with other Samaritans about her well experience with Jesus. I believe she developed the confidence and courage to witness to people from other cultures and different traditions after identifying her Jeremiah 29:11 identity. What made this woman phenomenal was her readiness to change, put down the water jug, and accept her Jeremiah 29:11 assignment to witness to others about the goodness of Jesus. This woman is phenomenal because she had many obstacles and became a witness in an instant. It is time for you to do a water check. Where is your water coming from? Let me encourage you to make sure that Jesus is your water and spiritual source. My sisters, maybe you played this role as the Samaritan woman by failing to trust God in personal situations as a mother, wife, and with individual struggles. God wants you to put down your burdens and give everything to Him.

You do not have to remain the way you are. Let go of the obstacles you tolerated. Believe and declare that Jesus is at your well, supplying all your needs. Taste your water! *Taste and see that the Lord is good. Oh, the joys, of those who trust in him* (Psalm 34:8). Share your water with somebody. Today, share your water with someone. You were created on purpose with a purpose. Begin your treasure hunt by operating in the joy of the Lord. *The joy of the Lord is your strength* (Nehemiah 8:10).

Still Point Moment: This woman is phenomenal because she made herself available to serve Jesus at the well and the people in her community. Most of all, she wanted to taste the living water Jesus was talking about. Jesus is where you are and wants you to have His gift of Living Water! Women of God, are you tired of the traps of sin? It's time to get in the plans God has for You! It's time to stay on the path of righteousness. It's time to get and stay in the word of God. It's time to establish systems of success! How can you stay on this path? You have to walk by faith and trust God!

Still Transition Affirmation: God cares about me. *For I know the plans I have for you," says the Lord. "They are plans for good and not for disaster, to give you a future and a hope (*Jeremiah 29:11*).*

Say yes to the living water that gives spring to eternal life. Share the living water experience with others by sharing the fruits of the spirit. The plans that God has for you include His promises and protection. God promises to love and protect you because you are a reflection of His image, gifts, and talents. You have to believe God cares and is in your path no matter what your situation looks like. Put down your water jugs and move forward in the Jeremiah 29:11 plans for you.

God's Plan for Women: Know Your Worth

Still Point: *I waited patiently for the Lord to help me, and he turned to me and heard my cry (*Psalm 40:1*). (2) He lifted me out of the pit of depair, out of the mud and the mire. He set my feet on solid ground and steadied me as I walked along. (3) He has given me a new song to sing, a hymn of praise to our God. Many will see what he was done and be astounded. They will put their trust in the Lord.*

Your testimonies can help someone to trust in the Lord. The Lord will set your feet on solid ground once you get into His presence. Let me encourage you to put your trust in the Lord this season.

John 8:3 *As Jesus was speaking, the teachers of religious law and Pharisees brought a woman they had caught in the act of adutery. They put her in front of the crowd.(4) "Teacher," they said to Jesus, "this woman was caught in the very act of adultery. (5) The law of Moses says to stone her. What do you say?" (6) They were trying to trap him into saying something they could use against him, but Jesus stooped down and wrote in the dust with his finger. (7) They (the crowd) kept demanding an answer so He stood up again and said, "All right, stone her. But let those who have never sinned throw the first stone! (8) Then he stooped down again and wrote in the dust. (9) When the accusers heard this, they slipped away one by one, beginning with the oldest, until only Jesus was left in the middle of the crowd with the woman (8) Then he stooped down again and wrote in the dust. (10) Then Jesus stood up again and said to her, "Where are your accusers? Didn't even one of them condemn you?" (11) "No, Lord," she said. And Jesus said, "Neither do I. Go and sin no more."*

The Pharisees brought a woman caught in the act of adultery before the people; however, the person she was caught with was not brought forward. This woman is nameless, but she had some obstacles. Jesus began to write in the sand. What do you think Jesus wrote in the sand with his finger? Do you think He wrote the name of person she was caught with in the act? Do you think He listed the accusers' sins? What Jesus wrote in the sand made the accusers walk away and leave the woman alone.

This woman's obstacle led to a life of adultery. Her punishment according to the law of Moses was death. This woman is phenomenal because she was brought to Jesus by the Pharisees. The Pharisees put her in front of her accusers and the crowd. However, Jesus did not reject this woman but, instead, accepted her repentance. This woman instantly was made whole.

Remember, the crowd will either crowd you or crown you. The crowd wanted to see her punished. You may have accusers who set you up only to use you for their amusement and evil purposes. In some cases, these are people with simialar problems and lusts. If people sin with you, they will sin with others. Therefore, you need to see yourself as valuable and know who you belong to. You belong to God and you need to see yourself as valuable.

The Pharisess brought this lady to Jesus and this worked in her favor. If you think about some situations you've experienced, the people who meant you evil are the ones that caused your prayer and praise life to increase. Once your prayer and praise increases, you will begin to look at yourself the way God sees you. Then you will understand your value.

Woman of God, start seeing yourself as valuable. I believe this woman instantly became whole in the presence of her accusers. Jesus is standing with you in the middle of the crowd while people want to throw stones, embarrass, and accuse you of doing the same things they are doing. The accusers used the Law of Moses to justify their reason to stone her to death (John 8:7). These accusers did not realize that Jesus was the new law and this woman who was brought to him belonged to him! What a reunion between Jesus and this nameless woman. She is now in the presence of Jesus.

You belong to Jesus and *there is no condemnation for those who belong to Christ Jesus* (Romans 8:1). *(2) For the power of the life-giving Spirit has freed you through Christ Jesus from the power of sin that leads to death. (3) The Law of Moses could not save us, because of our sinful nature. But God put into effect a different plan to save us. He sent His own Son in a human body like ours, except that ours are sinful. God destroyed sin's control over us by giving His Son as a sacrifice for our sins. (4) He did this so that the requirement of the law would be fully accomplished for us who no longer follow our sinful nature but instead follow the Spirit.*

Amen! You are chosen for a Jeremiah 29:11 assignment. God has plans for you because you belong to Him! My friend, be free at this moment from anything hindering you from enjoying your blessings and fulfilling your purpose. You are labeled as royalty (1 Peter 2:9), which means that you are valuable.

Still Point Moment: Repent. All it takes is a moment to acknowledge something that was wrong. Jesus, our mediator, looks beyond our faults and false accusations because He is the truth and light. You have a right to praise the Lord because He looks beyond what people say or thinks about you. Like this woman, go and sin no more in the plans God has for you.

Still Transition Affirmation: I will seek the Lord in trouble. *"Yet I will rejoice in the LORD! I will be joyful in the God of my salvation* (Habakkuk 3:18).

You are valuable and have purpose. Seek the Lord when you are in trouble because He is the maker of your Jeremiah 29:11 plans. God designed you with gifts and talents to be a blessing to yourself and others. Jesus is standing near you ready to comfort and meet your needs. Make room in your heart by forgiving yourself and others as you walk in your Jeremiah 29:11 plans.

God's Plan for Women: Be Royal

Still Point: *Who can find a virtuous and capable wife? She is worth more than precious rubies* (Proverbs 31:10).

You are royal because you are made in the image of God. The Queen of Sheba prepared for a quest and traveled with her best gifts to seek out King Solomon. She had heard about his reputation of being wise. She did not go alone. The scriptures describe the length, arrival, and experience with King Solomon.

(I Kings 10:1), *When the queen of Sheba heard of Solomon's reputation, which brought honor to the name of the Lord, she came to test him with hard questions. (2) She arrived in Jerusalem with a large group of attendants and a great caravan of camels loaded with spices, huge quantities of gold, and precious jewels. When she met with Solomon, they talked about everything she had on her mind. (3) Solomon answered all her questions; nothing was too hard for the king to explain to her. (4) When the queen of Sheba realized how wise Solomon was, and when she saw the palace he had built, (5) she was breathless.*

She was also amazed at the food on his tables, the organization of his officials and their splendid clothing, the cup-bearers and their robes, and the burnt offerings Solomon made at the Temple of the Lord. (6) She exclaimed to the king, "Everything I heard in my country about your achievements and wisdom is true! (7) I didn't believe it until I arrived here and saw it with my own eyes. Truly I had not heard the half of it! Your wisdom and prosperity are far greater than what I was told. (8) How happy these people must be! What a privilege for your officials to stand here day after day, listening to your wisdom!

(9) The Lord your God is great indeed! He delights in you and has placed you on the throne of Israel. Because the Lord loves Israel with an eternal love, he has made you king so you can rule with justice and righteousness." (10) Then she gave the king a gift of nine thousand pounds of gold, and great quantities of spies brought in as those the queen of Sheba gave to Solomon. (13) King Solomon gave the queen of Sheba whatever she asked for, besides all the other

---

customary gifts he had so generously given. Then she and all her attendants left and returned to their own land.

Solomon built a Kingdom with the blueprints that belonged to his father, King David. The Queen of Sheba heard of Solomon's reputation and it led her to seek out Jerusalem. She had a plan before making the trip. First, she wrote a list of questions. Second, she arranged for special gifts for King Solomon. Therefore, she arrived with many valuable gifts, prepared questions, and tests to exchange with Solomon. Solomon did receive the gifts, questions, and tests with answers. During this visit, King Solomon returned the favor with gifts and hospitality for her attendants. The Queen of Sheba realized how wise Solomon was and when she saw the palace he had built (I King 10:5), she was breathless. She was also amazed at the food on his tables, the organization of his officials and their splendid clothing, the cup-bearers and their robes, and the burnt offerings Solomon made at the Temple of the Lord.

When initiating a relationship, there should be an exchange of the Word of God, thoughts, kind words, conversations, gifts, fellowship, and food to develop and discover similarities and differences.

Lessons learned from the Queen of Sheba: The Queen of Sheba sought out wise builders of the Kingdom. She responded to Solomon's reputation (2nd Chronicles 9:1) and learned more than what she imagined. According to 1 Kings 10:9, the Queen of Sheba learned about God's eternal love and discovered Solomon's leadership was righteous. Four lessons to learn from Queen of Sheba are 1) seek out wise builders of the Kingdom 2) test those of interest 3) be generous and 4) ask questions.

1. **Test those of interest.** Reputation is important; therefore, it is important to keep some things to yourself. The Queen came up with hard questions. Ask individuals of interest questions to decide if they are worthy enough to be your company.

2. **Seek wisdom builders.** You need to know people or seek out people valuing their Jeremiah 29:11 plans.

3. **Be generous.** The Queen came with a large group of attendants and a great caravan of camels loaded with spices, huge quantities of gold, and precious jewels (2nd Chronicles 9:1). What are some gifts you have to offer someone of interests?

4. **Seek the Lord.** Step out of familiarity and seek after God's wisdom. Know people that seek after their Jeremiah 29:11 assignments.

Overall, the Queen of Sheba had a plan. Let me encourage you not to move without a plan. You need a plan in place to know where you are going and how long you are going to stay. The Queen of Sheba had a revelation of God's eternal love after she sought out on a quest towards Solomon. Her eyes were opened when she saw the palace and Temple of the Lord. And she was amazed at the food on his tables, the organization of his officials and their splendid clothing, the cup-bearers and their robes, and the burnt offerings Solomon made at the Temple of the Lord (2nd Chronicles 9:4).

Then the Queen of Sheba and all her attendants left and returned to their own land (2nd Chronicles 9:12b). This woman is phenomenal because as a wealthy and independent ruling queen she planned a quest to meet an extraordinary king. She strategized and thought of hard questions to ask Solomon. Her intended goal was to test Solomon with her gift of wisdom and knowledge; however, he answered her questions, riddles, and exchanged communication that left her amazed and breathless. She prepared the best gifts, treasures, and spices that represented her country's best!

This unknown named Queen of Sheba and King Solomon exchanged gifts and treasures; but, most of all, the queen exalted the name of the Lord! She realized that it was the God of Israel, Isaac, and Abraham that had blessed Solomon and the people. I can imagine Solomon giving the Queen of Sheba an exquisite tour of Jerusalem's Temple of the Lord and explaining the history of his father King David and relationship with the Lord. I believe when the Queen of Sheba traveled back to her country, she began to testify of all the things the Lord was doing in Jerusalem. Therefore, you need to understand your life is a testament of God's blessing to other people.

Your reputation and testimony can lead others to Christ and help them to discover their Jeremiah 29:11 purpose.

In the book of Matthew 12:42, Jesus says, *"The queen of Sheba will also rise up against this generation on judgment day and condemn it, because she came from a distant land to hear the wisdom of Solomon. And now someone greater than Solomon is hear-and you refuse to listen to him.*

The Queen of Sheba's deed is mentioned because of her quest for instruction, her willingness to listen and apply new meaning to her life and her country. In the Jeremiah 29:11 plans for your life, you have to return to God, repent, and live in God's prosperous will. Let me encourage you to remain in the courts of the vineyard.

Let me also encourage you to seek the Wisdom of God. The Jeremiah 29:11 plan for your life is to stay connected to the vine during test and trials! Understand that the water, birds, fish, mountains, land, and everything God created is designed to bless you in your quest for instructions from the Lord. Seek ye first the kingdom of God, and God will add to you! God will add flame to your oil because you are called to be a light to the world. Remember to share your water and gifts with others accordingly. Grace and peace to you! Continue to walk in the Jeremiah 29:11 plans!

Still Point Moment: *You will show me the way of life. Granting me the joy of your presence and the pleasures of living with you forever* (Psalm16:11). You are royal according to the Jeremiah 29:11 plans for you. You have a purpose to fulfill and a responsibility to build the Kingdom of God. It is important that you model this lifestyle in your home and relations with people to fulfill their purpose as well. You have gifts and talents to help others reach their next level in life. Let me encourage you to know your worth. Remember, Jesus knows your worth and it's never too late to turn to God.

Still Transition Affirmation: Let God be magnified. *Give your burdens to the Lord, and He will take care of you. He will not permit the godly to slip and fall* (Psalm 55:22).

God wants you to stay connected to Him through prayer, meditation, and Bible study. Listening to wisdom is a key principle in the plans God has for you.

God's Plans for Women: Victory!

Still Point: *Put on your sword, O mighty warrior! You are so glorious, so majestic! You are so glorious, so majestic! In your majesty, ride out to victory, defending truth, humility, and justice. Go forth to perform awe-inspiring deeds* (Psalm 46:3-4).

Victory is part of you Jeremiah 29:11 plans! Victory is given to you to withstand and overcome the personal battles and competitions forming against your success. This section is about victory and using your gifts and talents to help others combat!

"Victory At the Hands of a Woman"

In the book of Judges 4:4, Deborah, the wife of Lappidoth, was a prophetess who had become a judge in Israel. (Judges 4:6) *One day she sent for Barak, son of Abinoam, who lived in Kedesh in the land of Naphtali. She said to him, "This is what the Lord, the God of Israel, commands you. Assemble ten thousand warriors from the tribes of Naphtali and Zebulun at Mount Tabor. (7) I will lure Sisera, commander of Jabin's army, along with his chariots and warrior, to the Kishon River. There I will give you victory over him." (8) Barak told her, "I will go, but only if you go with me!" (9) "Very well," she replied, "I will go with you. But since you have made this choice, you will receive no honor. For the Lord's victory over Sisera will be at the hands of a woman." So Deborah went with Barak to Kedesh.*

Deborah

Your Jeremiah 29:11 identity may involve leading people into victory. Deborah's assignment was to tell Barak a message from the Lord, *"This is what the Lord, the God of Israel, commands you."* The lessons learned from Barak and Deborah include understanding the instructions for your purpose and your children's purpose. The plans God has for you affect the generations of today and the future. Therefore, it is important to understand the instructions to win the battle so you can have the victory!

Deborah was a judge and prophetess. According, to I Corinthians 14:3, *But one who prophesies is helping others grow in the Lord. (4) A person who speaks in tongues is strengthened*

---

*personally in the Lord, but one who speaks a word of prophecy
strengthens the entire church.*

     Deborah was a prophetess chosen by God to strengthen the
Israelites. Deborah preformed this duty as a judge, leader,
intercessor, and message deliver for the Israelites. Deborah was
phenomenal because she marched with Barak, a warrior, in the Lord's
battle. Her gift brought wisdom and direction from the Lord to the
battle fields. In the Jeremiah 29:11 plans God has for you, your plans
may be to march with someone with waver faith to help them fight or
bring strength to their battle.

     Deborah's husband was named Lappidoth. God had plans for
Lappidoth as the husband of Deborah. What a confident husband
Lappidoth must have been to trust his wife. What an encouragement
he must have been for Deborah as she went to work as a judge to
settle many disputes of the Israelites. What does this say about
Lappidoth's character? He was obedient to God and supported
Deborah's call to be a judge and prophetess.

Barak

     One day Deborah had a victory message to give to Barak. She
clearly gave him the message from the Lord. However, Barak
responded with his own sense of self and asked Deborah to come.
Barak's obstacle was unbelief. Deborah led an army of unbelievers.
As a prophet, she spoke the word from the Lord to Barak, and Barak
did not receive it. The Israelites had continuous cycles of unbelief,
disputes, battles, and leaders, including judges that would bring them
to victory. Barak may have adapted to the cycle of revolving doors
that the Israelites experienced. I can imagine Deborah and Barak
strategizing the victory to defeat Sisera.

     Barak was a warrior; but why did he ask Deborah to come
along? Was he worried about losing this battle? Did he hear Deborah
say? God wants you to trust His message and plans for you. You have
to make room in your heart to trust the Lord.

Sisera

     Who was Sisera? *Sisera was a commander of the army that
oppressed the Israelites. After Ehud's death, the Israelites again did*

what was evil in the Lord's sight *(Judges 4:1). (2) So the Lord handed them over to King Jabin of Hazor, a Canaanite king. The commander of his army was Sisera, who lived in Harosheth-haggoyim. (3a) Sisera, who had nine hundred iron chariots, ruthlessly oppressed the Israelites for twenty years.*

Get Ready

Then one day Deborah said to Barak, *"Get ready! Today the Lord will give you victory over Sisera, for the Lord is marching ahead of you." So Barak led his ten thousand warriors down the slopes of Mount Tabor into battle (Judges 4:15).* When Barak attacked, the Lord threw Sisera and all his charioteers and warriors into a panic. Then Sisera and leaped down from his chariot and escaped on foot. Let me encourage you that God is marching ahead of you. God will throw your enemy off during the battle. God will give you the advantage and capacity over your enemy. *(16) Barak chased the enemy and their chariots all the way to Harosheth-haggoyim, killing all of Sisera's warriors. Not a single-one was left alive. This battle was in the hand of God and the power came from God.*

Jael

(17) Meanwhile, Sisera ran to the tent of Jael, the wife of Heber the Kenite, because Heber's family was on friendly terms with King Jabin of Hazor. (18) Jael went outside to meet him, "Come into my tent, sir. Come in. Don't be afraid." So he went into her tent, and she covered him with a blanket. (19) "Please give me some water," he said. "I'm thirsty." So she gave him some milk to drink and covered him again. (20) "Stand at the door of the tent" he told her. "If anybody comes and asks if there is anyone here, say no." (21) But when Sisera fell asleep from exhaustion, Jael quietly crept up to him with a hammer and ten peg. Then she drove the tent peg through his temple and into the ground and so he died. (22) When Barak came looking for Sisera, Jael went out to meet him. She said, "Come and I will show you the man you are looking for." So he followed her into the tent and found Sisera lying there dead with the tent peg through his temple. Jael put the nail right through the head of the enemy.

This victory had a strategy. You have to know how to defeat your enemy with a plan. Jael was a phenomenal woman in place with the necessary courage, skills and talents to complete the battle. Barak chased Sisera, but he couldn't catch up with him. This chase led Sisera to Jael's court. Jael recognized that Sisera was the enemy, and invited him in her tent. She recognized that he was tired and gave him some milk to relax him instead of water. Jael knew that she only had one chance to end Sisera. With just one blow, she drove the tent peg through his temple and into the ground (Judges 4:23). She quietly went out of her tent and met Barak to show him that the battle was now over. Her skill was used to execute the enemy.

How did Jael know that giving Sisera milk instead of water would give him comfort? She knew that he was the enemy and had only one chance. Plus, Jael was skilled to use the nail. Your skills, gifts, and talents can help you and the people you are assigned to overcome situations.

The place where you stand in the battle may determine where your best skills, gifts, and talents will be used for the victory. God has people assigned to you to lead, guide, and intercede on your behalf. In the army of the Lord, you can defeat the enemy that's been attacking your tribe—meaning family and community. You can have victory over your situations when you work, fight, pray and agree with other believers. While in the battle, God will destroy the enemy whether he/she is positioned in the back, middle, or front. However, the mind and heart of the person that waits on God's plan will be strategically ready and expectant for the victory.

You can expect victory when you are interceding on the Lord's side. You can believe God has chosen you to win the battle. Let me encourage you to know that you are chosen to win every battle when you are on the Lord's side. God receives the honor when the battle is won. God will give you the wisdom to get ready for your Jeremiah 29:11 plans and purpose.

The children of Israel experienced victory unified as an army of the Lord. This victory was the first victory with the tent peg blow to the head by a woman. Generations later, the next victory happened when Jesus was nailed to the cross, pierced in his side, and died on the cross. Christ's resurrection is the fulfillment of the plans God has for us. It's the blood of Jesus that protects us from the weapons formed by our enemies. Victory comes when we allow God to fight our battles and the reward is a new position.

Deborah is phenomenal because she led the Israelites to their victory. Jael is phenomenal because she used her skills to make Sisera comfortable to the point that it put him to sleep. I can imagine that she appeared to look friendly and trustworthy. Let me encourage you that God has given you the necessary skills and tools to conquer the enemy. These phenomenal women were mighty in battle from beginning to end. There is a Deborah and Jael in each of you to use wisdom to win in every battle.

Still Point Moment: Take a moment to reflect on your situation. Do not worry if you cannot catch the enemy. God has somebody chosen to take care of the enemy. Let me encourage you to appreciate your skills because God has plans for your skills and talents according to His purposes. God will equip you for challenges and battles because your gifts work according to God's purposes.

Still Transition Affirmation: The Lord is my refuge. *The LORD is a shelter for the oppressed, a refuge in times of trouble (Psalm 9:9).* God is your refuge and all you have to do is seek God's wisdom to understand your purpose and when there is a shift in your condition.

Section 3: Chosen for Ministry Still Point Reflection

You are chosen to have victory and to be a witness for God's glory. God has chosen you to have victory over your enemies. Deborah, a prophetess and judge, interceded for Israel's victory from their enemies. In the plans God has for you, you may have to march and battle for victory. Barak was a warrior and leader of the Israel army and received the Lord's message from Deborah. However, Barak asked Deborah to march with their army. Deborah was on the battlefield with the Israelites. I believe she was praying for God to guide the victory and give the soldiers strength in the battle. Deborah was God's messenger and warfare leader. God is leading you to your victory. Don't worry about chasing your enemy. The enemy always runs out of places to hide and ends up on Jael's court.

Jesus is in the Jeremiah 29:11 purpose of your life and He's ready to transform your life like the women previously mentioned. Make room in your heart, home, mind, and time to be still for Jesus. These chapters presented victorious women. Trust God as you continue to journey towards your Jeremiah 29:11 purpose. Keep in mind how Mary, the sister of Lazarus, sat at the feet of Jesus while her sister Martha prepared a meal. Mary also cried on and wiped her tears off Jesus' feet after He turned Lazarus' situation around.

Mary's faith in Jesus' allowed her to become a follower of Christ. Like Mary, the Samaritan Woman realized that Jesus was the living water and brought people to Him. At times, our position is to bless Lord like the nameless woman who anointed Jesus body. The disciples did not understand what this nameless woman was doing, but Jesus revealed it to them. Remember that everyone is not going to understand your worship, however Jesus knows. Nameless women are in the Bible, but their deeds are memorable. They followed Christ when they realized that He had plans for them. You can be nameless when you do something nice for others.

Today's victories lead to tomorrow's victories for the next generations. You are chosen to be God's witness. Mary Magdalene, Salome, and Mary are phenomenal women because they were dedicated to their calling until the end and these women were chosen to give the report that Jesus is alive. The woman caught in the act of adultery was brought to Jesus. Amen! This woman's life was no longer the same after she encountered Jesus. I believe this woman was healed and made whole just like the woman with the issue of blood, Mary Magdalene, and YOU. Victory is yours. God has crowned you with victory in the Jeremiah 29:11 plans for you. You are chosen to have victory; be followers of Jesus, witnesses, royal, and always be ready to fight in the battle of the Lord!

Your foundation is built on God's purpose
Share your water
Drink His Water
Eat and walk fruitful
There are fruit actions to my purpose
Be a witness

SECTION 4:
THE MINISTRY
OF MOTHERHOOD

God's Plan for Women: Cry Out!

Still Point: *"Show me the path where I should walk, O Lord; point out the right road for me to follow* (Psalm 25:4). *Lead me by your truth and teach me, for you are the God who saves me. All day long I put my hope in you* (Psalm 25:5).

Will the real mothers please stand up? Being a mother is a ministry that involves being a caretaker. God's plan for mothers is to nurture, love, and protect children. It's not easy to be a mother; however, you have to let the Lord lead you by His truth and teachings. As mothers and caretakers, you have a responsibility to train the children in the ways of the Lord because there is a Jeremiah 29:11 seed within them that has to be nurtured, loved, and protected. There are times when you have to cry out for your children. In this section, you will read about women who faced trails in their positions as mothers. Many of the women you are about to read about stood alone and cried out to the Lord. Even when you cry or face situations that challenge your faith, God wants you to have hope all day and stand up.

Sometime later, two prostitutes came to the king to have an argument settled (I Kings 3:16). (17) *"Please, my lord,"* one of them began, *"this woman and I live in the same house. I gave birth to a baby while she was with me in the house.* (18) *Three days later, she also had a baby. We were alone; there were only two of us in the house.* (19) *But her baby died during the night when she rolled over on it.* (20) *Then she got up in the night and took my son from beside me while I was asleep. She laid her dead child in my arms and took mine to sleep beside her. (21) And in the morning when I tried to nurse my son, he was dead! But when I looked more closely in the morning light, I saw that it wasn't my son at all." (22) Then the other woman interrupted, "It certainly was your son, and the living one is mine." "No," the first woman said, "the dead one is yours, and the living one is mine." And so they argued back and forth before the king. (23) Then the king said, "Let's get the facts straight. Both of you claim the living child is yours, and each says that the dead child belongs to the other. (24) All right, bring me a sword." So a sword was brought to the king. (25) Then he said, "Cut the living child in two and give half to each of these women!" (26) Then the woman who really was the mother of the living child, and who loved him very much, cried out, "Oh no, my lord! Give her the child, please do not kill him." But the other woman said, "All right, he will be neither yours nor mine; divide him between us!" (27) Then the king said, "Do not kill him, but give the baby to the woman who wants him to live, for she is his mother!"*

A real mother cries out

Solomon and the case of the two mothers can be a relevant story to many women. Solomon did not judge these women based on their backgrounds but tested their love and ministry connection to the baby that lived. This story reveals the obstacles of lifestyles and truth. In this case one woman wanted something that the other woman treasured. The scripture points out that these women share a few things in common besides being mothers. These women worked as prostitutes and lived together. They were arguing over the living child's life. Solomon, in position as the judge, asked for the facts to assess the situation; however, he used wisdom to determine the real mother.

First, Solomon asked for the sword. Then, he used the sword to reveal who was the real mother. The real mother was willing to sacrifice her status as a mother to save her son from the sword so that the baby could live. Have you ever cried out for your children? Have you and your child ever been in harm's way or been tricked by someone you knew? Have you ever lived with or experienced a relationship with somebody who has tried to switch the principles you instilled in your children? As mothers, we have a responsibility to cry out, pray, and cover our children. I believe Solomon asked for the sword because he discerned who the real mother was.

Biblically, the sword is revealed as the word of God. The sword also is symbolized as the truth and protection. Solomon knew how to spiritually reveal the real mother. He used the sword to symbolize the truth. The mother that cried out was willing to sacrifice raising her child so that he could live. She knew her baby had a purpose. It's a mother's duty to nurse, teach, coach and guide children into their purpose. Like the mother willing to let the baby die and be divided, there is always someone on the prowl to switch your blessing into a curse. How does a real mother stand up? A real mother stands up "by crying out," for the child to live. Let me encourage you to face the facts of your situation. The mother of the child that died had to face the facts of living with the reality of making funeral plans; however, this reality would not be the end of her mother ministry. God still had turn-around plans for this mother. Always remember that God is not finished with you. You have to be willing to get more Word in you to have a relationship with God and understand the Jeremiah 29:11 path and plan.

A real mother stands alone

For both women, the ministry of being a mother had just begun to unfold as the mother's world becomes the baby's world. That's why it is important to be a Godly woman as a mother, caretaker, minister, teacher, trainer, coach, and friend. A mother that cries out has only two choices: stand alone or surround themselves with good people. Surround yourselves and your children with people who want your children to live. There will be individuals who come into your life who will try to switch or turn your children only to leave you with a dead child and results. These switchers are people who have rolled over on their own babies and are covering up their mistakes with lies, deception, and manipulation. These things have led to their child's death or living with the results of neglect. The individuals with switcher mindsets want to rob your children from their inheritance and keep them from any advancements and future success. Watch out for these switchers! These switchers operate as evil forces and competitors who want your blessings and even your children. This experience only confuses individuals. It's important for you to recognize that switchers are a part of the adversary's plan to divide, kill, steal, and destroy.

It has always been the devil's plan to kill, steal, and destroy God's promise and Kingdom. How do you protect your children from the harm and dangerous plans of the enemy? Let me encourage you to stand up. God has given you the victory to win in your situation. Revelation is the result of praying and seeking God. You can recognize switchers and dividers through their actions. You may have to end ties such as relationships, friendships, and social media connections after you've experienced set-ups such as lies and unexplainable drama. The act of crying out brings your desperation to God. You allow God to work through your situation.

II Corinthians 12:9, *"Each time" He said, "My gracious favor is all you need. My power works best in your weakness."*

Let me encourage you to stand alone and cry out. It's through your weakness that God's Wisdom and Power are revealed. Your world is your children's world; therefore, you have a responsibility to prepare your children to discover their purpose. Allow God to be your Healer in the loss of a son or daughter. Most of all, trust God in the plans to use you to become a caretaker/mother to the children He sends in your path to know their Jeremiah 29:11 plans and purpose. Be encouraged and know that God is not finished with you yet!

Still Point Moment: Being a mother is a ministry. Therefore, you have to be still and hear the wisdom of the Lord. Be a mother that protects her children. Be a mother that cries out for her children to live. In the Jeremiah 29:11 plans, there will be seasons in your life that you have to cry out and stand alone. During this alone time, hear from the Lord, find comfort in the Lord, spend time with the Lord, and stand up for the Lord just as Solomon. Whether your situation leaves you feeling full or empty, *God never abandons us* (II Corinthians 4:9)! Let me remind you that you are purposely designed to have victory in your situation.

Still Affirmation: I do not walk alone. *Those who plant in tears will harvest with shouts of joy* (Psalm 126:5). God is with you even in tough situations giving you the strength you need to walk toward your purpose. You have to hold on to your hope and faith that all things are working towards the Jeremiah 29:11 plans. Some days may seem harder than others, but you must believe that not one tear you cry is wasted. God is harvesting your tears that you may reap shouts of joy in the morning. Therefore, you must understand that you are never alone because God will plant every tear you cry. That's how close God is to you.

God's Plan for Women: Save the Generations

Still Point: *The humble will see their God at work and be glad. Let all who seek God's help live in joy* (Psalm 69:32). *For the Lord hears the cries of his needy ones; he does not despise his people who are oppressed (33).*

Take a moment to notice God at work and be glad. While you're waiting and receiving, be humble in the plans God has for you. Begin to realize that God works in your weakness according to your purpose. Therefore, you don't have to prove anything to people because God knows your purpose and plans. God will send people in your life to protect you from harm. Thank the Lord for the doulas to take you to your next levels.

Exodus 1:(18) *Then Pharaoh, the king of Egypt, gave this order to the Hebrew midwives, Shiphrah and Puah:* (16), *"When you help the Hebrew women give birth, kill all the boys as soon as they are born. Allow only the baby girls to live."(17) But because the midwives feared God, they refused to obey the king and allowed the boys to live, too. (18) Then the king called for the midwives, "Why have you done this?" he demanded. "Why have you allowed the boys to live?" (19) "Sir," they told him, "the Hebrew women are very strong. They have their babies so quickly that we cannot get there in time! They are not slow in giving birth like Egyptian women." (20) So God blessed the midwives, and the Israelites continued to multiply, growing more and more powerful. (21) And because the midwives feared God, he gave them families of their own.*

God has blessed you and your purpose. Therefore, you can stand strong against your adversary. Did you know that God has made you to be stronger than your enemy? God will send you a midwife or doula to help you arrive in your purpose. A doula is a person who guides and helps women during their pregnancies until the birth of the baby. Many times, doulas will remain close and support the mother during the changes that takes place with pregnancy. While rising above adversity, God will bless you with strength that is stronger and wiser than that of your oppressor.

The Hebrew doulas are an example of women of purpose. These Hebrew doulas feared the Lord. Their obstacle was to keep the Hebrew baby boys alive while there was a law in place to kill them. You need people in your life that fear the Lord. The bravery of these women kept the generations alive. I believe these women saved as many baby boys as they could. Also, I believe they knew how to out-smart Pharaoh's employers. This made people following Pharaoh's orders the footstool of the doulas. This implies that your enemy is setting you up to be blessed. Therefore, sit near Jesus, and the Word says He will humble your enemy and make them your footstool (Luke 8:42-43; Psalm 110; Acts 2:34-35).

You are designed to be a blessing to others. Like these doulas and midwives, there are people in your life to protect you from harm and danger. These women risked their lives to save a generation. Wisdom allowed these women to fear God and not the Egyptians. Let me encourage you to put your trust in God who knows the plans for you!

Treasure in the Basket

(Exodus 2:1) During this time, a man and woman from the tribe of Levi got married. (2) The woman became pregnant and gave birth to a son. He was a beautiful child in God's eyes (Acts 7: 20). *She saw what a beautiful baby he was and kept him hidden for three months.* (Hebrew 11:23) *It was by faith that Moses' parents hid him for three months. They saw that God had given them an unusual child, and they were not afraid of what the king might do.* (Exodus 2:3) *But when she could no longer hide him, she got a little basket made of papyrus reeds and waterproofed it with tar and pitch. She put the baby in the basket and laid it among the reeds along the edge of the Nile River. (4) The baby's sister then stood at a distance, watching to see what would happen to him. (5) Soon after this, one of Pharaoh's daughters came down to bathe in the river, and her servant girls walked along the riverbank. When he princess saw the little basket among the reeds, she told one of her servant girls to get it for her.*

The Hebrews' generation had a common goal of saving their sons from death. The story of Moses begins with phenomenal Hebrew midwives, Shiphrah and Puah. Shiphrah and Puah feared God, refused to obey the king's orders, and allowed the Hebrew newborn boys to live. God blessed the midwives because of their fearlessness and faithfulness. I believe Shiphrah or Puah crossed the path of Jochebed. Jochebed was the birth mother of Moses. She showed their fearlessness and faithfulness by hiding Moses from the order of Pharaoh to *"Throw all the newborn Israelite boys into the Nile River. But you may spare the baby girls* (Exodus 1:22)."

I can imagine the mother, Jochebed, prayerfully sought God's wisdom as to how to save her son's life. Jochebed was an experienced mother having been pregnant with two older children named Aaron and Miriam. I can see Jochebed hiding her pregnancy and keeping it a secret. I can see her staying out of sight and praying for God's wisdom. God is revealed in Jochebed's situation. God revealed to Jochebed how to keep the baby hidden and alive with a plan. This plan included how to build a basket that would float on the river and navigate in the closeness of Pharaoh's daughter.

Jochebed and Miriam learned Pharaoh's daughter's schedule by watching the palace. I can imagine Jochebed making the basket and studying the water currents that would lead Moses to Pharaoh's daughter. I can imagine, during the night, Jochebed and Miriam were at the river strategizing and getting their timing right for Moses' safety.

The time came when Pharaoh's daughter got ready for her bath. I can imagine Jochebed had hesitations when it was time to let go. Jochebed knew the time had come to trust God. I believe Jochebed got as close as she could to the palace and waited for Pharaoh's daughter to bathe in the river. The moment came when God took control of this situation once the mother let the basket go. By faith, Jochebed waited for the Nile to flow steadily before placing the basket on the water surface.

As Jochebed set the basket in the water, Miriam followed the basket as planned. Jochebed watched and Miriam followed her baby brother's basket as it floated on top of the water. I can imagine Miriam praying for the basket to stay on the surface of the water. Miriam remained fearless and faithful to follow her brother.

This mother is phenomenal because she wanted her son to live. This mother prayed, hid her child from Pharaoh's plan, and worked in precise timing with God's plan. She waited for God's plan to know how and when to plant her son in his purpose.

When you pray, you have to be prepared for God's answer. Therefore, you need to make room in your heart to receive your answer. Moses' parents had to trust God. God's purpose is revealed as the plan works itself out. This family is immediately reunited. Jochebed is phenomenal because she listened to God's wisdom. This fearlessness is shown in Miriam's courageous poise as she followed the basket and approached Pharaoh's daughter. Miriam's purpose was to be a witness to her baby brother's arrival to his purpose.

Moses' birth was a secret to the Egyptians but not to God. Jochebed pushed Moses' basket in the direction of Pharaoh's palace. Your purpose is to trust God and your gift is designed to bless someone else. Jochebed believed Moses had a purpose to live. She risked her life so that he could live. This mother prayed for a special covering for her baby to live and not die by Pharaoh's sword.

Miriam's assignment was critical as she stood in the distance and watched her baby brother. Miriam's purpose was to obey her mother and approach the princess. What a reunion. I can imagine Jochebed building Miriam's courage to approach the princess with words to say. Miriam found her mother and together they went to the princess. Moses was saved by the princess, but Jochebed was paid to nurse her son (Exodus 2:9).

God saves, recovers, and reunites your blessings back to you once you've demonstrated that you can let go. I can imagine the joy Jochebed had bonded with her son, because she knew her time would be limited. I believe Jochebed taught Moses the principles and promises of God. She exposed him early to God's ways and teachings. She demonstrated God's purpose and the history of their ancestors. She instilled the hope and identity of the blessings of Abraham. Jochebed had to return Moses to the princess (Acts 7:21-22) once he grew. When she took him back to the palace, where Joseph once knew as, she planted him in his purpose. I'm sure Miriam supported her mother and showed courage. When Jochebed had to let go of her son this second time, Moses had an identity. I believe Jochebed let go confidently as Moses walked away from his mother, sister, and culture.

Moses excelled and benefited from the knowledge and skills taught by his natural mother. While living with his adopted family, Moses was a good student who learned and adopted skills during his palace apprenticeship that would prove to be an advantage as future leader. Jochebed, Miriam, Shiprah, and Puah remained faithful to the God of Israel, Isaac, and Jacob. You are not just raising ordinary children. Your children have a purpose. The principle of unity is important in the plans God has for you to save a generation like these phenomenal women.

Still Point Moments: My sisters, do not allow conditions of the world to throw you off your path. Trust God; and train your children to know the ways of the Lord. Like Shiprah and Puah, you have to fear the Lord. It's our responsibility to save our children from the hands of the enemy and oppressor. Like Jochebed, we have to trust God and have a plan for our children to live and not die! Then, when it's time to let our children go, we can confidently know that the purpose planted in them will not depart from him. After you give birth, turn your children over to the Lord! Remember that you are raising generational leaders to build up the Kingdom of God. Our prayers are the covering that protects them in their paths when we have to let them go. You are responsible for planting your children in their purpose. It's time to plant Kingdom seeds into our children. As mothers, you have to nurse your child's purpose by feeding them with the Word of God.

Still Transition Affirmation: I will not fear. *I trust in God, so why should I be afraid? What can mere mortals do to me?* (Psalm 56:11). God wants you to trust Him in every situation. God's promises are written for you to trust and have hope that the conditions around you are controlled by Him.

You have to make room in your heart for faith. Faith requires you not to fear but to be content in the situation that God is working out for you. You have to align your faith and belief to the Jeremiah 29:11 plans for you.

God's Plan for Women: Test Your Children

Still Point: *The Lord is king! Let the nations tremble! He sits on His throne between the cherubim. Let the whole earth quake (Psalm 99:1)!*

Have faith in the Lord when things run out. God will supply the things you need through your work and faith. You have to make room in your heart to hear the Word of the Lord and become a servant to do His Will. This is your season to listen to Jesus and do what He says! Let me encourage you to invite Jesus into your life and have a party.

John 2: 1- 12: Water to Wine
The next day Jesus' mother was a guest at a wedding celebration in the village of Cana in Galilee. (2) Jesus and his disciples were also invited to the celebration. (3) The wine supply ran out during the festivities, so Jesus' mother spoke to him about the problem. "They have no more wine," she told him. (4) "How does that concern you and me?" Jesus asked. "My time has not yet come." (5) But his mother told the servants, "Do whatever he tells you." (6) Six stone waterpots were standing there; they were used for Jewish ceremonial purposes and held twenty to thirty gallons each. (7) Jesus told the servants "Fill the jars with water." When the jars had been filled to the brim, (8) he said, "Dip some out and take it to the master of ceremonies." So they followed his instructions. (9) When the master of ceremonies tasted the water that was now wine, not knowing where it had come from (though, of course, the servants knew), he called the bridegroom over. (10) Usually a host serves the best wine first," he said. "Then, when everyone is full and doesn't care, he brings out the less expensive wines. But you have kept the wine until now!" (11) This miraculous sign at Cana in Galilee was Jesus' first display of his glory. And his disciples believed in him. (12) After the wedding he went to Capernaum for a few days with his mother, his brother, and his disciples.

Woman of God, when you know the plans God has for you and your children, you will have faith like Mary to test them. When you know the plans God has for you and your children, you will take them with you, introduce them to others, give them assignments that develop their gifts, and know their circle of friends. Mary is phenomenal because she knew her purpose as a mother as well as her son's. Yet, Mary gave her son an assignment to get some more wine.

First, Mary spoke with Jesus about the problem of the wine running out. Let me encourage you to talk to Jesus about your problems. Then, you need to listen to Jesus about the plans God has for you. Mary knew the plans God had for Jesus because she accepted her assignment as his mother. Most of all, Mary believed in her son. She knew Jesus was ready because of the many things she taught Him as well as what she witnessed Him do and say. As a mother, she spent her life preparing and protecting him for His ministry. She knew her Son had wisdom and knowledge of His Heavenly Father. Most of all, she knew when it was the right time to reveal Him. Mary was obedient and knew it was time for Jesus to be revealed at the wedding celebration. However, the deeper revelation was that Mary knew Jesus was the new wine and the fruit the people needed.

Second, Jesus was obedient to His mother. Mary told the servers, *"Do whatever he tells you* (John 2:5)." In this statement, Mary is stating a message that would prepare generations to come, *"to do whatever he tells you us to do,"* and get ready for new wine and drink and eat of the fruit from his branch according to Isaiah 11:1.

Isaiah 11:1 reads, *Out of the stump of David's family will grow a shoot-yes, a new Branch bearing fruit from the old root. (2) And the Spirit of the Lord will rest on him-the Spirit of wisdom and understanding, the Spirit of counsel and might, the Spirit of the knowledge and the fear of the Lord. (3) He will delight in obeying the Lord. He will never judge by appearance, false evidence, or hearsay. (4) He will defend the poor and the exploited. He will rule against the wicked and destroy them with the breath of his mouth. (5) He will be clothed with fairness and truth.*

Third, be a servant of the Lord and follow His instructions. You have not discovered or experienced "the best" God has for you. Through love and compassion, Mary gave her son an assignment. Why? Mary had spent her life preparing and protecting His purpose so she knew it was time to let go. It is time for you to have a party and rejoice with others about what the Lord has done. Also, Mary had concern about these newlyweds' party. This concern signifies that Mary wanted the best for this marriage. She brought this concern to Jesus and wanted Him to meet the needs of the bride and groom.

The servants listened to Jesus. Jesus is the bridegroom that has the best waiting for you! He doesn't serve the best wine first and then later bring out the less expensive wine. Jesus is the new root from the old root. This means His fountain source will never run out! Like Mary, we have to plant the plans God has for us in our children. Most of all, we have to have faith in our children when their assignment comes and let them go.

Let me encourage you Woman of God, if we just keep our faith and do what Jesus says, Jesus will be our source of supply! Your miracle is in the room when Jesus is present! "Invite Jesus" and put Him first in your life. God said if we seek Him, we will find Him—that's a promise from God!

Still Point Moment: In the plans God has for you, there is no run-out! You can rejoice that God wants you not to worry about your finances if it's getting close to zero or when it looks like you're running out. Like the wedding party, Jesus is in the mist of your relationship. All you need to do is bring your concern about yourself and others to Him.

Still Transition Affirmation: God is my helper. *But the Lord is my helper. The Lord is the one who keeps me alive!* (Psalm 54:4).

God is your helper and the one who keeps you alive in the Jeremiah 29:11 plans for you. God will help, protect, and guide you with wisdom and life in your Jeremiah 29:11 plans. The purpose that lives inside you needs to be connected to God constantly to fulfill its duty.

God's Plans for Women: Rejoice Together

Still Point: *Shout with joy to the Lord, O Earth* (Psalm 100:1). *(2) Worship the Lord with gladness. Come before Him, singing with joy.*

Let's take a look at two phenomenal women, Mary and Elizabeth. Both women encountered the same angel to receive the Jeremiah 29:11 plans God had for them. In their situation, the angel interrupts their plans to give them 'good news.' The angel Gabriel appeared suddenly to both women and gave them new revelations. Get ready to receive and rejoice about the Jeremiah 29:11 plans and purpose God has for you this season.

Luke 1:5 *It all begins with a Jewish priest, Zechariah, who lived when Herod was king of Judea. Zechariah was a member of priestly order Abijah. His wife, Elizabeth, was also from the priestly line of Aaron.* (6) *Zechariah and Elizabeth were righteous in God's eyes, careful to obey all the Lord's commandments and regulations.* (7) *They had no children because Elizabeth was barren, and now they were both very old.* (24) *Soon afterward his wife, Elizabeth, became pregnant and went into seclusion for five months.* (25) *"How kind the Lord is!" she exclaimed. "He has taken away my disgrace of having no children!"*

The plans God has for you includes you rejoicing with others. Rejoicing with others includes making connections and spending time with others. Elizabeth rejoiced because she received the Word and message from Gabriel. Look at Elizabeth's response. (Luke:1:25) *"How kind the Lord is!" she exclaimed. "He has taken away my disgrace of having no children!"* She rejoiced because she had been expecting an answer to her prayers. When you're expecting God to answer your prayers, you need to make room in your heart to receive it in God's timing.

Let me encourage you to begin to seek God's wisdom to prepare to conceive the answer. *Elizabeth, became pregnant and went into seclusion for five months* (Luk2 1:24). God will work through your faith when you are expecting something. When you've been waiting and finally get your answered prayer, you may have to seclude yourself from your crowd and familiar places. At times, familiar places in your new level and revelation can hinder your season because you have to protect the early trimesters of your receiving and conceiving. Suddenly, after the angel visited, Elizabeth's and Zechariah's situation changed. Together, they needed to become one to support the arrival and upbringing of their son, John.

Let's look at Elizabeth's barren situation. Bareness for a season or walk can lead you to your Jeremiah 29:11 plans. No matter how your situation may look, you have an appointed time to give birth to something great. You will learn Elizabeth secluded herself and Zechariah couldn't talk during her pregnancy. Most of all, you will discover how not to give yourself a label because God is moving in your life. Elizabeth is phenomenal because she had faith and hope that she would be a mother. The phenomenology lesson we learn from Elizabeth is to stay ready! Stay ready for your blessing! Stay ready to be blessed! Stay in the light of faith, and don't get discouraged and label yourself barren. The plans God has for you are to prosper you and build His Kingdom. Always be ready for a new word and answer. Discover the Jeremiah 29:11 purpose for your life because God is not finished with you. Do not think you're too old or young to be blessed. There is an anointing on your life and God is going to get the glory.

Pregnant with a Purpose

Elizabeth became pregnant and went into seclusion for five months (Luke 1:24). Luke 1:26: *In the sixth month of Elizabeth's pregnancy, God sent the angel Gabriel to Nazareth, a village in Galilee, (27) to a virgin named Mary. She was engaged to be married to a man named Joseph, a descendant of King David. (28) Gabriel appeared to her and said, "Greetings, favored woman! The Lord is with you!" (29) Confused and disturbed, Mary tried to think what the angel could mean. (30) "Don't be frightened, Mary," the angel told her, "for God has decided to bless you! (31) You will become pregnant and have a son, and you are to name him Jesus. (32) He will be very great and will be called the Son of the Most High. And the Lord God will give him the throne of his ancestor David. (33) And he will reign over Israel forever, his Kingdom will never end!" (34) Mary asked the angel, "But how can I have a baby? I am a virgin." (35) The angel replied, "The Holy Spirit will come upon you, and the power of the Most High will overshadow you. So the baby born to you will be holy, and he will be called the Son of God.*

(36) *What's more, your relative Elizabeth has become pregnant in her old age! People used to say she was barren, but she's already in her sixth month. (37) For nothing is impossible with God."* (38) *Mary responded, "I am the Lord's servant, and I am willing to accept whatever he wants. May everything you have said come true." And then the angel left. Mary stayed with Elizabeth about three months and then went back to her own home,* St. Luke 1:56.

Gabriel shared a revelation with Mary that, *"Nothing is impossible for God."* Mary response to her new assignment changed instantly that, *"I am a servant of the Lord, and I am willing to accept whatever He wants."* Mary journeyed to visit Elizabeth in her sixth month and stayed with her for three months. All together this calculates to nine months. I believe Mary was there to give Elizabeth the support she needed since Zechariah could not talk. What do you think Elizabeth and Mary shared during their time together? Together, Mary and Elizabeth were in the same place, i.e. secluded and preparing for their births and the ministry of their children. Understand that your gifts and talents are designed to bless somebody else. I can imagine that this was no regular family visit when Mary arrived at Elizabeth's place. This visit was a faith visit to rejoice, pray, and prepare their children and themselves for the work of the Lord. For support they turned and became doulas and caretakers for each other.

The Angel Gabriel (Luke 1:19), brought Zechariah good news about his wife Elizabeth. Gabriel told Zechariah, *"for he will be great in the eyes of the Lord. He must never touch wine or hard liquor, and he will be filled with the Holy Spirit, even before his birth."* (Luke 1:15) Therefore, it should not be any surprise that, *"at the sound of Mary's greeting, Elizabeth's child leaped within her, and Elizabeth was filled with the Holy Spirit (Luke 1:41)."* This leap in the womb confirms the Word growing inside Elizabeth. She became full of the Holy Spirit. Elizabeth responded to her once barren situation with praise.

Luke 1:(42) *Elizabeth gave a glad cry and exclaimed to Mary, "You are blessed by God above all other women, and your child is blessed." At this moment, Elizabeth immediately confirms to Mary of her conception of Jesus, and begins to praise God by stating, (43) "What an honor this is, that the mother of my Lord should visit me!*

Elizabeth revealed and confirmed Mary's new status as the mother of Jesus. Both of these women are phenomenal because of the commitment to believe the report of Gabriel and accept their assignment. Accepting your assignment is a major element to understanding your role and responsibility to your Jeremiah 29:11 plans. I can imagine Elizabeth opening up her arms and hugging Mary with warmth.

Sisters, it's time that we begin to support each other with the gifts that are within us because my gift is for you/others and yours is for me/others. I understand there are many social roles you portray during the day; however, for the Kingdom you have a new hat to wear.

Today, you will receive a hat. You have to put on a hat and become a doula, meaning that there comes a time when you have to support and help someone push out their gift. There are going to be times when you don't want to wear your doula hat, but you have to just do it!

Women, we need to spend time with each other in order to exchange, strengthen, and share our fruit, and also to receive knowledge and learn new information. Mary's visit to Elizabeth was part of her assignment to become wife to Joseph and mother to Jesus. Both of these women are phenomenal because of the commitment to believe the report of Gabriel and accept their assignment. Accepting your assignment is a major element in understanding your role and responsibility in your Jeremiah 29:11 identities and ministries to help others. In this season, you need to keep your faith on duty.

At times, we get caught in the web of routine and our faith gets caught when it seems our prayers are not answered. What are you operating in: fear or faith? Fear will paralyze your faith walk. Fear will keep you barren and in the dark. Zechariah's fear and unfaithfulness responded to Gabriel's message. The lesson we learn from Zechariah is not to respond in fear to God's plan. Responding in fear could abort your purpose. In Zechariah's case, his fear response could have aborted his purpose as a father and John's purpose to baptize Jesus.

Today, begin to operate in great expectation that God will supply all your needs (Philippians 4:13). Be encouraged, and do not give yourself a label. Also, don't accept the labels people may give you because God is not finished with you (Jeremiah 29:11). Therefore, keep an open mind to receive blessings from the Lord.

We carry the weight of burdens, shame, secrets, and doubts when conditions appear barren. How are we supposed to respond to God when our faith is blocked because of the web of insecurities? The answer is to keep your faith and walk in hope. When results appear barren or in the dark, *"Jesus said, 'I am the light of the world. If you follow me you won't be stumbling through the darkness, because you will have the light that leads to life* (John 8:12)."* Take back your thinking, and get it out the web of insecurities. Wait on God to make your move like Elizabeth and Mary. He is working on moving in your Jeremiah 29:11 plans.

Become doulas and sisters. When our gifts are not supported, we will rival with ourselves and others in the situation which can cause competition. Competition causes division and misery which can only end when you begin to praise God. What is competition? In this text, competition is defined when your competitor wants what you have or your belt/what you hold. Someone in your crowd wants what you have and your influence without going through what you've been through. Your competitor wants your blessing by tricking or fighting you. Your competitor may be your family or church member(s), co-worker(s), or stranger(s). The competitor always has a plan to taste or take what you have. Therefore, it is important for you to discern people by the fruit (Galatians 5:22-23) they bring to the table. It is important for you to bring and share good news with others to make their spirit rejoice. Have faith this season because God works through your faith. Accept your assignment and protect the early trimesters with people you can rejoice with and trust.

Still Point Moment: Both women received their new assignments as mothers and first teachers for their children. You have an assignment for yourself and children. Discover God's plan and purpose for you. God wants you to trust His Word when you don't see His plans.

Still Transition Affirmation: I can do all things through Christ. For I can do everything with the help of Christ who gives me the strength I need (Philippians 4:13).

You can do all things through Christ when you make room in your heart to receive what God has for you. The purpose that lives within you is designed to stand and liberate yourself and others. Your purpose is connected to your spirit to hear from God to guide you and others into the Jeremiah 29:11 assignment.

God's Plan for Women: Pray

Still Point: *O Lord, hear me as I pray; pay attention to my groaning* (Psalm 5:1). *(2) Listen to my cry for help, my King and my God, for I will never pray to anyone but you. (3) Listen to my voice in the morning, Lord. Each morning I bring my requests to you and wait expectantly.*

This section will explore Rebekah's determination to complete Esau and Jacob's Jeremiah 29:11 plans and purpose. Rebekah's marriage family and struggles directed her to pray. Get ready to receive revelation for the plans and purpose God has for you this season.

(Genesis 25:21) *Isaac pleaded with the Lord to give Rebekah a child because she was childless. So the Lord answered Isaac's prayer, and his wife became pregnant with twins. (22) But the two struggled with each other in her womb. So she went to ask the Lord about it. "Why is this happening to me?" she asked. (23) And the Lord told her, "The sons in your womb will become two rival nations. One nation will be stronger than the other; the descendant of your older son will serve the descendants of you younger son." (24) And when the time can, the twins were born. (25) The first was very red at birth. He was covered with so much hair that one would think he was wearing a piece of clothing. So they called him Esau. (26) Then the other twin was born with his hand grasping Esau's heel. So they called him Jacob. Isaac was sixty years old when the twins were born.*

Isaac prayed with the Lord to give Rebekah a child because she was childless. The Lord answered and blessed Rebekah. Rebekah's obstacle was that she felt a struggle in her womb. Rebekah's prayer was attached to questions about her pregnancy. It was only then that God revealed her situation of carrying twin boys. The descendants of the older nation will serve the younger generation and each will rival with one another. This prayer during her pregnancy is the only recorded revelation of Esau and Jacob's plan. God revealed to her that the sons in her womb would become two rival nations and the younger son would be stronger than the oldest.

This was Rebekah's revelation (Genesis 25:23): *"The sons in your womb will become two rival nations. One nation will be stronger than the other; the descendants of your older son will serve the descendants of your younger son."* This revelation from God gave Rebekah direction for raising her sons.

Delivery

Rebekah's delivery of the twins was described as Esau separating from the womb first with Jacob grasping his heel. Could Jacob's hold to his brother's heel reveal his strength and fight to be first? Think about it. Rebekah had no break between their births because of Jacob's latch to Esau. This latch to Esau's heel can illustrate Jacob's strength as a baby. Was this the beginning of the rivalry between the brothers? Was this Jacob's race for the birthright? Throughout their childhood, I can imagine Rebekah praying to God throughout Esau and Jacob's lives. Isaac's revelation of Esau and Jacob is not recorded; however, both boys were treated separately different. From the womb to birth, the twins continued to struggle with each other.

An important lesson we learn from Rebekah is that you may begin to experience a struggle in your seasons of development but you have to ask God to reveal to you the gifts you are carrying. Rebekah thought she had a normal pregnancy until the struggle was too much to bear. Just as she called to God for a revelation of the struggle in her womb, you can ask God to reveal the plans for you and your children. This revelation led to Rebekah's obedience to the revelation and prepared Jacob for the labor. I can imagine that Rebekah never forgot about her condition during her pregnancy, labor, and delivery of the twins. Most of all, she did not forget about the revelation received from her prayer to God. In the plan God has for you, write down your prayer requests and journal your thoughts or revelations that may have been deposited in your spirit. If you receive a vision, write it down so you can set goals to achieve it.

Competition out of the Womb

Let's examine Jacob and Esau's childhood relationship. Sibling rivalry causes constant competition for attention from parents.

Even though Rebekah knew the revelations of her twins, she kept a close eye on Jacob. I can imagine that Esau noticed Rebekah's favor towards Jacob. I believe Jacob desired after the birthright and strategized every opportunity to trade it with Esau. I can imagine under the tent Jacob competed with Esau to be the first one done eating, walking, talking, and showing love and respect to their parents. Also, the twin brothers knew each other's strength and weakness. However, Esau became a skillful hunter and a man of the open fields while Jacob was the kind of person who liked to stay at home (Genesis 25:27). One day Jacob knew that one day Esau would be hungry after hunting.

(Genesis 25:29) *One day when Jacob was cooking some stew, Esau arrived home exhausted and hungry from a hunt. (30) Esau said to Jacob, "I'm starved! Give me some of that red stew you made." (31) Jacob replied, "All right, but trade me your birthright for it." (32) "Look, I'm dying of starvation!" said Esau. "What good is my birthright to me now?" (33) So Jacob insisted, "Well then, swear to me right now that it is mine." So Esau swore an oath, thereby selling all his rights as the firstborn to his younger brother. (34) Then Jacob gave Esau some bread and lentil stew. Esau ate and drank and went on about his business, indifferent to the fact that he had given up his birthright.*

Sibling rivalry causes competition and struggles to build in the relationships. Birthrights are generational blessings and assignments that require responsibility. Esau gave up his birthright because he did not respect the practices of hard work and responsibility. Jacob had a strategy to take Esau's birthright package. Jacob fed Esau while in his weakness. Why didn't he offer his brother just the stew in his weakness? Notice that Jacob used this opportunity to get his need met. So how long did Jacob strategically plan to trade the birthrights? Unknowingly, Jacob was operating in his purpose. On the other hand, Esau should not have given up his birthright so easily.

Jacob had been clutching Esau's heel since birth, and he always had a plot to get the birthright; but, Rebekah had the revelation. The parents had a role in developing the sibling rivalry. Now let's take a look at the parents, Rebekah and Isaac. (Genesis 25:28) Isaac loved Esau in particular because of the wild game he brought home, but Rebekah favored Jacob. Why did Rebekah favor Jacob? Did Rebekah's revelation cause her to favor Jacob? What happens when parents show favor? Favoritism causes division and struggle between siblings as the child starves for parental attention.

Rebekah's Plan

Rebekah continued to serve her husband in his old age and when he became sightless. She seemed to be at the right place at the right time to position Jacob for the blessing. Once she heard that Isaac was ready to release the blessing, she knew where to find Jacob and acted with quickness and swiftness. The moment came for Rebekah to prepare Jacob for his purpose. Rebekah disguised Jacob to receive the blessing in the presence of the Lord. Rebekah's plan to disguise Jacob (Genesis 27:6-17) was a faith action from her revelation.

Genesis 27:1 When Isaac was old and almost blind, he called for Esau, his older son, and said, "My son?" "Yes Father?" Esau replied. (2) "I am an old man now," Isaac said, "and I expect every day to be my last. (3) Take your bow and a quiver full of arrows out into the open country, and hunt some wild game for me. (4) Prepare it just the way I like it so it's savory and good, and bring it here for me to eat. Then I will pronounce the blessings that belong to you, my first born son, before I die." (5) But Rebekah overheard the conversation. So when Esau left to hunt for the wild game, (6) she said to her son Jacob, "I overheard your father asking Esau (7) to prepare him a delicious meal of wild game. He wants to bless Esau in the Lord's presence before he dies (8) Now, my son, do exactly as I tell you. (9) Go out to the flocks and bring me two fine young goats. I'll prepare your father's favorite dish from them. (10) Take the food to your father; then he can eat it and bless you instead of Esau before he dies." (11) "But Mother!" Jacob replied, "He won't be fooled that easily. (12) What if my father touches me? He'll curse me instead of blessing me." (13)"Let the curse fall on me, dear son," said Rebekah. "Just do what I tell you. Go out and get the goat."

Rebekah felt this was the only opportunity to position Jacob even though he had to be disguised and trick Isaac. She positioned Jacob for the blessing by disguising him as Esau. She told Jacob about the plan and he trusted his mother. She acted quickly to disguise him in Esau's best clothes, made a pair of gloves, strip of goat's skin for his neck, and cook the food (Genesis 14-18). She prepared Isaac's favorite dish and gave Jacob directions to serve his father and receive the blessing. I can imagine Rebekah listening and praying outside the tent as Jacob presented the meal to Isaac. Jacob received the blessing from his father. This blessing included the promise of God from generations to generations. Jacob received the blessing before Esau returned. How long did it take for Esau to hunt and get ready? Why didn't Esau move fast about this time and season? Let me encourage you to act fast with a plan to receive the plans God has for you. Most of all you have to have a heart ready to receive. Esau lacked a healthy work ethic. Esau had a gift to hunt, but why did it take him so long? Having a healthy and 'go get it' attitude is important in the plans God has for you. Rebekah and Jacob probably was aware that Esau was easily distracted and lacked drive.

Rebekah's Last Plan

At the time of the blessing, Esau was married to two Hittite women. I believe Rebekah knew Esau's wives would not appreciate the blessings. Let's look at Esau's situation as he grew from son, brother to husband. Later on, (Genesis 27: 34-35) *at the age of forty, Esau married a young woman named Judith, the daughter of Beeri the Hittite. He also married, Basemath, the daughter of Elon the Hittite. (35) But Esau's wives made life miserable for Isaac and Rebekah.* The results of Jacob's tricks and competition made Esau bitter (Genesis 27: 36), caused him to have a breakdown (Genesis 27:38), induced hate, and a desire to kill his brother Jacob (27:41). Esau did not make good decisions. On the other hand, Jacob was always ready to take on advice. In the plans God has for you, be ready to take wisdom from somebody listening to God. Most of all, be teachable and coachable. Have an attitude and work ethic for God's will to be done with an open heart. One more time, Jacob had to take his mother's advice. This time, Jacob would have to leave and run from his twin brother.

(Genesis 27:42) *But someone got a wind of what Esau was planning and reported it back to Rebekah. She sent for Jacob and told him, "Esau is threatening to kill you. (43) This is what you should do. Flee to your uncle Laban in Haran. (44) Stay there with him until your brother's fury is spent. (45) When he forgets what you have done, I will send for you. Why should I lose both of you in one day?"*

Once again, Rebekah experienced another obstacle. This time her obstacle was to keep her sons alive. Rebekah's quick actions were tested once she heard of Esau's threat to kill Jacob. She asked Isaac to bless Jacob's departure from Paddan-aram to the house of his grandfather, Bethuel, and to marry one of Laban's daughters (Genesis 28:1-2). Rebekah's last plans were to let go of Jacob. Yet did Rebekah realize that as Jacob, her beloved son, left for his safety, she would never see him again? As a mother, I can imagine that Rebekah struggled with not having the son she beloved around. I believe she wanted Jacob to have what God had planned for him. In order for Rebekah to have Jacob receive God's plans, she had to let him go. The plans God has for you require you to trust Him and let Him do the rest. Rebekah directed Jacob towards his path of destiny. I believe she did not stop praying for her sons. Esau wanted the blessing of Isaac, but he did not want to follow God's plan. Jacob wanted God's plan and the blessing. God wants to bless you and prosper you within the Jeremiah 29:11 plans.

Rebekah is phenomenal for her obedience to the revelation from God. From Rebekah's womb, Jacob struggled with his brother. Out of the womb, he was disguised to be his brother and later hid from and then reconciled with his brother. Once Rebekah received her revelation, she knew her purpose. Yet, the results led to competition between brothers during childhood and adulthood; but in the outcome, Israel shared the blessing with Esau. Rebekah's action plans for Esau and Jacob were all about the revelation of two nations. Rebekah gave Isaac and Jacob many orders to fulfill the revelation she received during her pregnancy.

You are the nation God revealed to Abraham, Isaac, and Rebekah. The struggle is over when we allow God to have His way. Rebekah influenced Isaac, Esau, and Jacob's lives. This struggle represents the delivery and birth of the blessings and promises from God to Abraham, Isaac, and Jacob. We are the nation through the blood of Jesus chosen to make peace with our brothers and sisters. Now, it's through Israel we receive these promises. We are connected to these promises. Now, Israel can make peace with his brother and live in peace among his people.

Still Point Moment: Believe that the struggle is over. We are a chosen nation to be the head and not the tail. Jacob made peace with his brother Esau. God will enlarge your territory in the Jeremiah 29:11 plans for you. Let me encourage you to bless those with whom you struggle. Jacob struggled with Esau from the womb. Now, we can live in peace with the one we once struggled with. There is victory in the struggle.

Still Transition Affirmation: God cares about me. And we know that God causes everything to work together for the good of these who love God and are called according to His purpose for them (Romans 8:28).

You are called according to God's purpose for His work. God wants you to work together with others to fulfill the Heaven on Earth assignment for Kingdom purposes. Those purposes include you using your gifts and talents for the purposes of spreading the hope message that God has plans for you and others.

God's Plan for Women: Position your Children

Still Point: *I come to you for protection, O Lord my God. Save me from my* persecutors-*rescue me* (Psalm 7:1*)!*

Let's take a look at another mother who positioned her son to receive the blessing and new position. Solomon was the son of Queen Bathsheba and King David. King David was old and had to name one of his son's king. Bathsheba had to listen to the Prophet Nathaniel to position Solomon as King and save his life.

Bathsheba learned about God because King David ministered to her when they lost their first child. I believe King David demonstrated to Bathsheba how Solomon should be raised knowing the Lord. I can imagine Bathsheba praying to God for wisdom in the raising of Solomon. You should always make time for God. God is the Father and creator of our seasons. Therefore, you need to pray and worship to get directions and instructions about the plans in store for you. Be committed to God's work and plan for your life. Also, be responsible to go in the direction God has planted you in with faith and confidence and receive your crown.

Wait for God

Adonijah decided to appoint himself king which became an obstacle in King David's plan for Solomon to succeed him. King David promised Bathsheba that Solomon would succeed him as king. But when King David became old, his son Adonijah decided to make himself king (I Kings 1:5). Isn't that just like the spirit of a thief to steal what has not been ordained for them? Responsibilities are given to complete assignments, tasks, and commitments. In the plans God has for you, there are going to be seasons when you will get tested and challenged and people become the obstacle. However, do not be afraid. God is with you.

Move on God's Plan

Let's look at the phenomenology of Bathsheba's role in Solomon's seat on the throne of King David. First, Bathsheba listened to Nathan the prophet report about Adonijah, Hagith's son, who made himself king (I King 1:11). Next, she had to learn from the prophet what to say to King David (I King 1:12) in order to receive his instruction for Solomon's position. Also, Bathsheba knew that she had to listen to Nathan the prophet's counsel to save her and Solomon's lives.

Second, she did not have time to rehearse the script to the plan from Nathan, she had to act quickly. Third, in her role as queen, when it was time to enter, she bowed to King David, and kept to the script. Fourth, she left when Nathan the prophet came in as planned. Fifth, she waited for her answer! While she waited, King David and Prophet Nathan counseled together about a plan for Solomon.

"Call Bathsheba." David said. So she came back in and stood before the king (I King 1:28). (29) And the king vowed, "As surely as the Lord lives, who has rescued me from every danger, (30) today I decree that your son Solomon will be the next king and will sit on my throne, just as I swore to you before the Lord, the God of Israel."

Sixth, Queen Bathsheba received her answer directly from King David. According to I Kings 1:34, Bathsheba bowed low before him again and exclaimed, "May my lord King David live forever!" Queen Bathsheba is phenomenal because she sought help and counsel in her obstacle. In the plans God has for you, it includes you preparing your children for Kingdom work and kingdom-ship. As a parent, you may have children who rebel against you or each other, but keep good counsel around you that will give you a report of what your children are doing when you're not looking. Consider Queen Bathsheba's response and wisdom when you face adversity or somebody trying to slip into your position or your children's position.

Queen Bathsheba was responsible for surrounding Solomon with the teaching necessary to become a successful king. Let me encourage you that you are responsible to set your children up to be blessed for their position. As a mother, you are your child's first teacher and promoter for their wealth. Wealth is birthed in your children. This is why you must train and test them. Give your children responsibilities, make them save their money in a savings account, and remain involved in their education. Surround your children with good counsel and people who will keep an eye on your children when you're not around.

Nathan the prophet knew that Solomon was to succeed David as King, while Adonijah, Hagith's son, was plotting to steal the throne. You want good people around you who will listen to God and not people. Bathsheba is phenomenal because she listened and stuck with the script to set her son, Solomon, on the throne. The story ends with Solomon as the successor.

Still Point Moment: Have you ever been in a situation similar to Bathsheba? Bathsheba had to respond to make sure Solomon received his crown. You are tagged with the promise of victory in the Jeremiah 29:11 plans that God has for you! You are tagged to be a blessing and a winner! Today, let your situation know that you will not support lack, defeat, and fear. You are empowered with gifts and talents to overcome any challenge in your life. Remember, after you defeat the giant, the reward is a new position. Receive your new position gracefully in the name of the Lord. Help others receive their crown as you continue to seek the Jeremiah 29:11 plans.

Still Transition Affirmation: God is on my side. The Lord is my strength and my song; He has become my victory (Psalm 118:14). Victory is yours when God is on your side.

God's Plan for Women: You are Chosen

Still Point: *God is our refuge and strength, always ready to help in times of trouble* (Psalm 46:1).

God spoke to Abram about the land that He was going to give his offspring. However, at this time Abram lived in Babylon and was not a father. In an act of faith, Abram and his family moved from his familiar land and set out for the land of Canaan. During their move they experienced many transitions in their family. Abram's wife, Sarai, was anxious and made the plans work for her. Did Abram remain faithful to God's promise? Did Abram share with Sarai about the conversations he had with God? What state of reality was Sarai in about becoming pregnant? To answer these questions, let's look at the phenomenology of Sarai/Sarah and Hagar.

(Genesis 16:1) But Sarai, Abram's wife, had no children. So Sarai took her servant, an Egyptian woman named Hagar, (2) and gave her to Abram so she could bear his children. "The Lord has kept me from having any children," Sarai said to Abram. "Go and sleep with my servant. Perhaps I can have children through her." And Abram agreed. (3) So Sara, Abram's wife, took Hagar the Egyptian servant and gave her to Abram as a wife. (4) So Abram slept with Hagar, and she became pregnant. When Hagar knew she was pregnant, she began to treat her mistress Sarai with contempt. (5) Then Sarai said to Abram, "It's all your fault! Now this servant of mine is pregnant, and she despises me, though I myself gave her the privilege of sleeping with you. The Lord will make you pay for doing this to me." (6) Abram replied, "Since she is your servant, you may deal with her as you see fit." So Sarai treated her harshly, and Hagar ran away.

Hagar

Hagar was Sarah's Egyptian slave. Hagar's obstacle was listening to Sarah. How did Hagar, an Egyptian slave get chosen for the responsibilities as a wife and surrogate mother? Sarah came up with a plan for Hagar to become Abraham's second wife with the hopes of having children through her (Genesis 16:2). Even though

Hagar was Abram's wife and pregnant, she was still Sarah's servant. Hagar understood that she was Abram's wife, but struggled with Sarah under the tent. Hagar's life experience had been arranged for her because slavery was all she knew. For example, Hagar experienced many trades throughout her life as a slave. Someone always made decisions and plans for Hagar's life. She had no voice about her life and this made her miserable.

Hagar wanted to be free from a life as a servant. I can image that she felt this marriage with Abraham would give her a status as a wife; however, she remained Sarah's mistress. I can imagine as Hagar lived in Sarah's tent, she prayed to rise above her slave status.

As Abram's second wife, Hagar's conceived baby became part of the blessing. Sarah treated Hagar harshly even though it was her plan to become a mother through Hagar. Sarah was not able to handle her plan effectively which left her more bitter and resentful toward Hagar. Can you imagine Hagar's position? She was getting treated like a slave, when she should have been treated as a wife.

The God Who Sees Me

Have you ever been in a Hagar situation? Maybe you were in a relationship with somebody and they used you to get their needs met? Have you ever been part of somebody's arrangement because you had what they needed? How did that make you feel after the person made changes to the arrangements? What did you learn from your situation? Did you run from the situation or did you continue with the contract?

One day, Hagar decided to run away. This experience led her to the desert. Pregnant and confused, Hagar ran from her situation. However, she received an encounter from the Lord. Did Hagar realize that God had plans for the baby she was carrying?

(7) *The angel of the Lord found Hagar beside a desert spring along the road to Shur.* (8) The angel said to her, *"Hagar, Sarai's servant, where have you come from, and where are you going?" "I am running away from my mistress,"* she replied. (9) *Then the angel of the Lord said, "Return to your mistress and submit to her authority."* (10) *I will give you more descendants than you can count."* (11) *And the angel also said, "You are now pregnant and will give birth to a son. You are to name him Ishmael, for the Lord has*

heard your misery. (12) This son of yours will be a wild one free and untamed as a wild donkey! He will be against everyone, and everyone will be against him. Yes, he will live at odds with the rest of his brothers." (13) Thereafter, Hagar referred to the Lord, who had spoken to her, as "the God who sees me," for she said, "I have seen the One who sees me!"

Hagar's revelation is that God sees! Like Hagar, you may be in a situation that has led you to a desert place; but, realize that God sees you. Arrangements and agreements can change between people; however, God sees everything. Hagar referred to the Lord as, "the God who sees me." What a revelation Hagar received in order to understand her situation. God will protect the Jeremiah 29:11 word you are pregnant with and deliver it in due season.

What has the Lord provided to you when you were ready to run away and give up? When Hagar was running, she had a plan and thought, but the angel of the Lord appeared to her and asked her, "Hagar where are you going?" The Lord will show up to direct you back on track to your purpose. Your gift and purpose is to bring results to someone's barren situation. Your purpose is to bring life to someone who's not producing. Your gift is designed to bless someone else. Sarah's barren results led her to use Hagar to produce Abraham a child.

Let's examine Sarah's position. Can you imagine Sarah's desires to be a mother? As a woman, have you ever prayed and prayed for results only to find yourself waiting? Dreams barren! Hope barren! Situations barren! Her hopes were to give Abram a child and have children through Hagar. How do you think Sarah felt when Hagar's pregnancy began to show? Did this lead to Sarah's harsh treatment towards Hagar? Why did Sarah become bitter to Hagar? Was Sarah ready for the arrangement that she planned to have children through Hagar?

(15) *So Hagar gave Abram a son, and Abram named him Ishmael.* The angel of the Lord revealed that God saw her misery and told Hagar to return and submit to Sarah. Hagar followed those instructions and gave birth to Ishmael. I believe God provided for Hagar when she returned and saw her situation differently and more responsibly. God will provide for you when you are ready to submit, forgive, and be guided into the plans for you. Be encouraged about

your situation because God sees and will reveal when you're ready to receive.

God Provides in Dry Places

(Genesis 21:8) *As time went by and Isaac grew and was weaned, Abraham gave a big party to celebrate the happy occasion. (9) But Sarah saw Ishmael- the son of Abraham and her Egyptian servant Hagar- making fun of Isaac. (10) So she turned to Abraham and demanded, "Get rid of that servant and her son. He is not going to share the family inheritance with my son, Isaac. I won't have it!" (11) This upset Abraham very much because Ishmael was his son. (12) But God told Abraham, "Do not be upset over the boy and your servant wife. Do just as Sarah say, for Isaac is the son through whom your descendants will be counted. (13) But I will make a nation of the descendants of Hagar's son because he also is your son." (14) So Abraham got up early the next morning, prepared food for the journey, and strapped a container of water to Hagar's shoulders, He sent her way with their son. And she walked out into the wilderness of Beersheba, wandering aimlessly.*

Sarah's perception of Hager was that she was her servant. It appears that as Ishmael grew, he stayed close by Abraham and Sarah. Also, Sarah became pregnant and gave birth to Isaac. I can imagine that Sarah had regrets about her first plan to become a mother through Hagar. Therefore, Sarah came up with another plan for Hagar and Ishmael. However, this time Sarah told Abraham to get rid of Hagar and Ishmael for good. Can you imagine Abram's position as a father? Ishmael and Isaac were his sons and Sarah wanted to separate the brothers for good. Abraham must have prayed because God gave him an answer. God told Abraham not to be upset and reminded him of the prophecies spoken over the sons. How do you think Abram was feeling as he prepared Hagar and Ishmael's long travel? How do you think Abram said goodbye to Ishmael?

Have you ever been made to leave a familiar place, a home or work place because of differences? Has anyone ever treated you harshly after you helped them a favor? How did that make you feel? Can you imagine how Hagar felt after Abram gave her bread and bottled water for a distant travel? Can you imagine how betrayed she felt after she submitted to Sarah's authority and put up with her bitterness over the years?

All Hagar had ever known was how to submit and serve others; she had never been free until her dismissal from Abraham's tent with her son Ishmael. I can imagine Abraham telling Hagar to trust God as he gave her some bread and water for the journey. I believe Abraham and Ishmael had a close relationship and saying good-by must have been hard. Hagar and Ishmael began their travel and new life together. However, the water that Abraham gave them for their journey ran out while they were in the wilderness.

Hagar's Wilderness

(Genesis 21:15) *When the water was gone, she left the boy in the shade of a bush. (16) Then she went and sat down by herself about a hundred yards away. "I don't want to watch the boy die," she said as she burst into tears. (17) Then God heard the boy's cries, and the angel of God called to Hagar from the sky, "Hagar, what's wrong? Do not be afraid! God has heard the boy's cries from the place where you laid him. (18) Go to him and comfort him, for I will make a great nation from his descendants." (19) Then God opened Hagar's eyes, and she saw a well.*

Can you imagine Hagar walking in the wilderness of Beersheba with Ishmael alone? Abraham provided an amount of bread and strapped a container of water on Hagar. However, the food and water ran-out. Hagar had no direction or destination in this journey to unpack and call home. While she wandered in the desert, the food and water ran out! She desperately began to search for water. For a moment, she had to put Ishmael down to search alone for water. She was determined to find water. In the plans God has for you, you may have to make desperate decisions to get the things you need. She heard the voice of the Lord direct her back to her son and then she saw a well. Let me encourage you to cry out to the Lord when you've done all that you can. God is concerned about the plans He has for you. Therefore, God is concerned about your run-out. It's through your run-out God is able to provide through your faith in Him.

Hagar is phenomenal because in her obstacle she had the courage to cry out. Hagar is a brave mother who travel through the wilderness and a determined woman to look for water alone in the wilderness. As we look at Hagar's situation, it's evident that God hears and responds to the cries of His children, just like He heard Ishmael's cries. God will speak to you and open your eyes so you can see what He has provided for you from Heaven. Hagar is a witness that God opened her eyes and provided a well for Ishmael. Hagar wanted her son to live and had to make a decision to leave him for a moment. Only then did God open her eyes. She immediately filled her water container and gave the boy a drink.

According to the scriptures, *God continued to watch over His seed because Ishmael lived. (20) And God was with the boy as he grew up in the wilderness of Paran. He became an expert archer (21) and his mother arranged a marriage for him with a young woman from Egypt.* Who do you think taught Ishmael archery? I believe his father, Abraham taught him and this teaching remained with him. After this study, how do you think influential women are considering this Sarah and Hagar situation? What about Abraham's position with Sarah and Hagar?

Let me encourage you to look at your situation knowing that God sees you and cares. Like Hagar, God wants you to stop running away from your situation and turn to Him. Believe that God sees and understands what you're going through, but you don't have to remain the way you are! You have the victory to overcome miserable situations. You do not have to run from your situation like Hagar. God is with you, and you are not alone! Submit your body, mind, and spirit to God so you can see yourself as God sees you. God revealed to Hagar that she was pregnant with a son, who would be heir to Abraham's blessing. Hagar received this revelation as hope for Ishmael's future. In the Jeremiah 29:11 plans God has for you, your plans are designed for you to have hope and prosper in your future. Therefore, God is near and ready to provide when you experience a run-out.

Still Point Moment: The plans God has for you are to have hope and prosper in your future. As a mother or caretaker, it is important to know the Jeremiah 29:11 plans for your children. God is concerned and will supply when you run-out or cry-out.

Still Transition Affirmation: God is faithful and will fulfill all He promises to you. The Lord is for me, so I will not be afraid. What can mere mortals do to me? (Psalm 118:6)

Have hope in the plans God has for you. God is faithful to meet your need while you discover and experience situations. Make room in your heart for hope, courage, confidence, and resolve to experience the fullness of promises for you. Wait with patience for the promises to be fulfilled for you.

Section 4: The Ministry of Motherhood Still Point Reflection

Being a mother is a ministry. You are uniquely covered as you face challenges. Like Elizabeth, the mother of John, God can turn your barren situation around. Elizabeth is phenomenal because she kept hope in her situation. Let me encourage you to have hope that your situation will change. Accept your Jeremiah 29:11 assignments like Mary, the mother of Jesus, and humble yourself. Like Elizabeth and Mary, Jochebed hid her pregnancy and birth of Moses from her community to keep him safe. God had a plan for the generations of Moses, John, and Jesus. You are designed to be a blessing to others and prepare the next generation for their Kingdom of Heaven assignment.

It's time to rejoice about the Jeremiah 29:11 plans and purposes God has for you!! It's time to give God the glory!! It's time to walk in victory!! Let's thank the Lord for the plans to be a blessing to others. Thank you Lord for the fruits of favor to taste and see how good You are! Thank you Lord for blessing us with the gifts and talents to dress the Kingdom and reflect your grace and glory. Thank you Lord for the phenomenal men and women you chose to change their situation from barren to bountiful, last to first, and the strength to wait and let go. Thank you Lord for the courage to watch, wait, and respond to the Jeremiah 29:11 plans for us! Amen.

Everything is possible through God. *Give all your worries and cares to God, for He cares about what happens to you* (I Peter 5:7). Clear your mind and heart of any obstacle that is worrying you. Fear and unbelief will block you from Heavenly benefits. Therefore, you have to make room in your heart to receive and understand the plans God has for you with faith. Continue to walk in the Jeremiah 29:11

plans, operate in faith, and believe with joy that everything is possible through God.

You were created in the Image of God
You have spiritual gifts
You have a Heaven of Earth assignment
You were made in the image of God
You were given the gift of life
This is your season to "Let go!"

CONCLUSION

God's Plan for Women: Walk in Victory

Walk in Victory as you begin a new season knowing that you are chosen by God to have a ministry as a woman, mother, wife, sister, aunt, teacher, or community leader. You have what it takes as a Woman of God to minister to yourself and family. You have a message to share with others about Jesus. My prayer is that you matured in Christ reading this book. Your faith unlocks the promises and plans God has for you. Continue to be encouraged and have hope in every situation. Let me encourage you to have hope in God's promises.

You don't have to remain the way you are because you are royal! Be encouraged, God is not trying to destroy you, but keep you. If you are suffering or feeling low, you have to learn how to trust in God. These men and women struggled, wrestled, and endured until they got it together. Let me encourage you to have faith as you go through your situation knowing the plans God has for you.

You have to grow and mature into the Jeremiah 29:11 plans. God has plans for everybody, no matter how old you are? God told Jeremiah, "I formed you in your mother's womb." Therefore, you have been ordained since before you were formed to conquer and have victory in your situations. The plans God has for us are designed to bring out the best in us. In this design, God will break us in love to keep growing and seeking Him. This process is for our good to reach our next level. God will work through and mend the broken pieces. God's strength will work through your weakness and build your faith.

This process involves God working and shifting within you to make your better for the Kingdom. My prayer is that this book planted you on the Jeremiah 29:11 plans and path and that the Word of God has grown deeper in you. It is also my hope that you understand your Jeremiah 29:11 identity as you go to your next level. God has plans for you to have divine hope and a future.

Your faith has been increased for the Jeremiah 29:11 identity, plan, and purpose for you and your family.

Be restored and have faith.

Be encouraged. Have hope in your situation like Elizabeth.

Stay in the plans God has for you by becoming a follower like Mary and the other women.

Serve and become a witness like the nameless woman at the well.

Cry out to the Lord like Hagar.

Have wisdom like Deborah.

Stay in the will of God.

Treasure God's instructions like Mary.

Recover like Eve.

Be royal like the Queen of Sheba.

Be prompted by faith to discover your Jeremiah 29:11 identity.

Be renewed and transformed like all the women who followed Jesus!

Walk with courage knowing that God has predestined you to have the victory.

You have what you need to walk in the plans God has for you.

Give encouragement to those that are going through difficult situations.

Take on your new strength and joy as you walk in your Jeremiah 29:11 identity.

REFERENCES

Beers, G., Beers, R., & Tyndale House Publishers (1996). *Touchpoint Bible: God's Word at Your Point of Need (New Living Translation)*. Tyndale House Publishing.

ABOUT THE EDITOR

Courtney Berry is the owner and editor-in-chief of Iron PROOF Editing Firm, a professional writing, editing, and proofreading company based in Washington, DC. IPEF offers a range of editorial services to businesses, students, authors, and other individuals seeking to sharpen their writing.

Prior to launching Iron PROOF, Courtney was a public school educator for over a decade and taught reading, writing, public speaking, middle school language arts, high school English, and English as a Second Language (ESL). Musically gifted, when not editing, she spends time composing choral music. She holds professional memberships in the Editorial Freelancers Association (EFA) and the American Copy Editors Society (ACS).

ABOUT
THE AUTHOR

Dr. Brandi Brown is the mother of three children, Carandus, Jr., Jamaia, and Imani. Her children are the inspiration of writing and completing the books, *Jeremiah 29:11 The Plans I Have for You, Woman: Walk in Victory!*; *Jeremiah 29:11 The Plans I Have for You, Man: Be Champions!*; *Jeremiah 29:11 The Plans I Have for You, Children and Families: Preparing the Next Generations!*

Dr. Brandi DeShawn Brown is an educator trainer and mentor of School Street-School Counseling and Consulting Services. School Street-School Counseling and Consulting Services which offers college and career awareness, race-relations presentations, and multicultural arts and mentoring designed for students, educators, and individuals and groups.

www.ingramcontent.com/pod-product-compliance
Lightning Source LLC
Chambersburg PA
CBHW030108070426
42448CB00036B/482